YORK
STREET ATLAS

Contents

Key map and Legend	3
City centre map	4
Map pages	6
Places of interest	21
Index to streets	24

GEOGRAPHIA

Geographia, part of John Bartholomew & Son Ltd, was founded over 70 years ago. This Geographia street atlas is one of a new and up to the minute series of street atlases, each one of which has clear easy to read mapping and a full street index.

The greatest care and attention is taken when we produce these atlases but, if you find any errors, we would be grateful to hear from you.

If you wish to send us information relating to this product, please contact:-

The Chief Cartographer,
Geographia Limited,
105/107 Bath Road,
Cheltenham,
Glos. GL53 7LE

© Geographia Ltd. 1988 LAL A/N609

First Edition 1988

Published by Geographia, an imprint of John Bartholomew & Son Ltd, Duncan Street, Edinburgh EH9 1TA.

Great care has been taken throughout this book to be accurate but the publishers cannot accept responsibility for any errors which appear, or their consequences.

Printed in Great Britain by John Bartholomew & Son Lt

KEY TO MAP PAGES

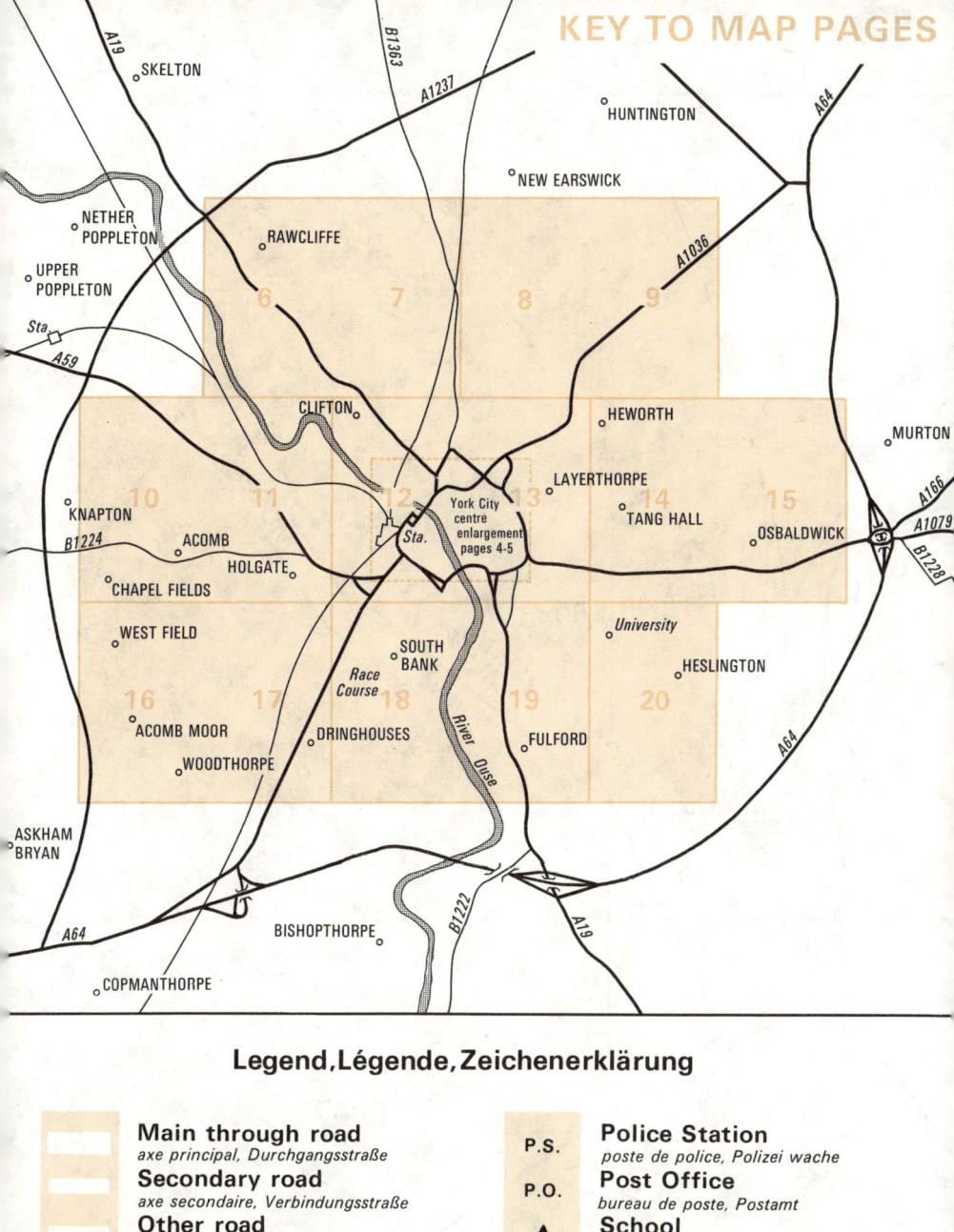

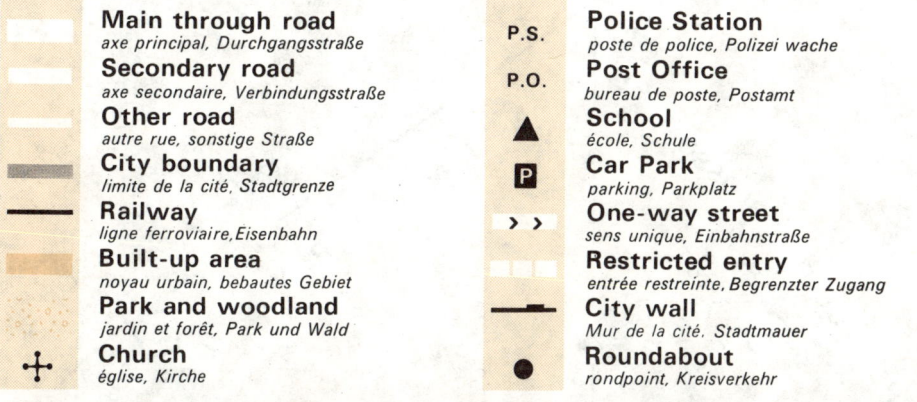

Map grid locations:
- 6: Rawcliffe area
- 7
- 8: New Earswick area
- 9
- 10: Knapton area
- 11
- 12: York City centre (Sta.)
- 13: Layerthorpe
- 14: Heworth / Tang Hall
- 15: Osbaldwick
- 16: Acomb Moor
- 17
- 18: South Bank / Race Course / Dringhouses
- 19: Fulford
- 20: University / Heslington

York City centre enlargement pages 4-5

Labelled places: Skelton, Huntington, New Earswick, Nether Poppleton, Upper Poppleton, Rawcliffe, Clifton, Heworth, Murton, Knapton, Acomb, Holgate, Layerthorpe, Tang Hall, Osbaldwick, Chapel Fields, West Field, South Bank, University, Heslington, Acomb Moor, Dringhouses, Fulford, Woodthorpe, Askham Bryan, Bishopthorpe, Copmanthorpe

Roads: A19, B1363, A1237, A64, A1036, A166, A1079, B1228, A59, B1224, B1222, A64

River Ouse, Race Course, Sta.

Legend, Légende, Zeichenerklärung

	Main through road — axe principal, Durchgangsstraße
	Secondary road — axe secondaire, Verbindungsstraße
	Other road — autre rue, sonstige Straße
	City boundary — limite de la cité, Stadtgrenze
	Railway — ligne ferroviaire, Eisenbahn
	Built-up area — noyau urbain, bebautes Gebiet
	Park and woodland — jardin et forêt, Park und Wald
✠	**Church** — église, Kirche
P.S.	**Police Station** — poste de police, Polizei wache
P.O.	**Post Office** — bureau de poste, Postamt
▲	**School** — école, Schule
P	**Car Park** — parking, Parkplatz
>>	**One-way street** — sens unique, Einbahnstraße
	Restricted entry — entrée restreinte, Begrenzter Zugang
	City wall — Mur de la cité, Stadtmauer
●	**Roundabout** — rondpoint, Kreisverkehr

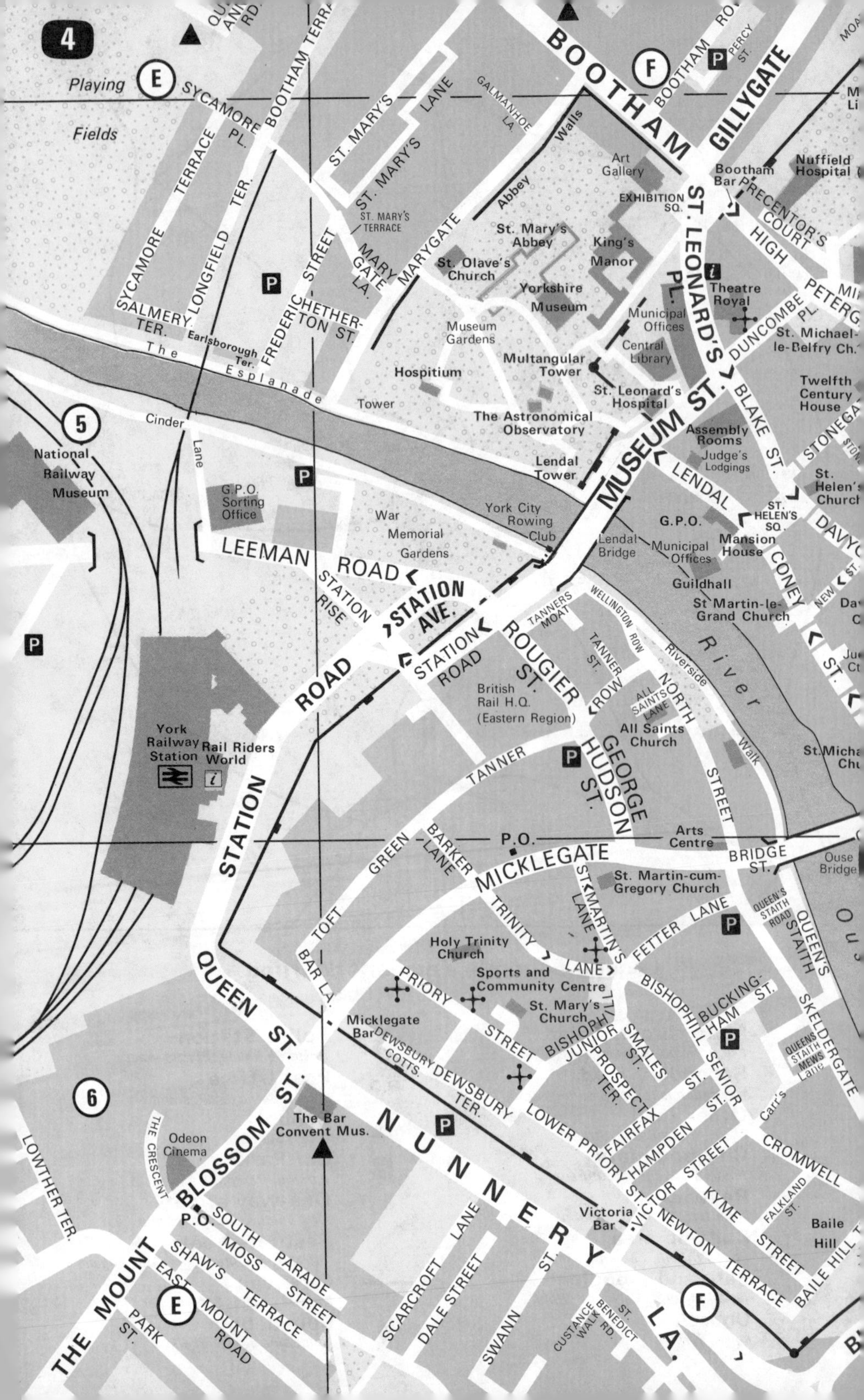
4
Playing Fields
E
F
5
6
Sycamore Pl.
Sycamore Terrace
Longfield Ter.
Bootham Terrace
Bootham
Bootham Row
Percy St.
Gillygate
St. Mary's Lane
St. Mary's
Galmanhoe La.
St. Mary's Terrace
Marygate La.
Marygate
Abbey Walls
Art Gallery
Exhibition Sq.
Bootham Bar
Nuffield Hospital
Precentor's Court
High Petergate
St. Mary's Abbey
King's Manor
St. Olave's Church
Yorkshire Museum
Theatre Royal
St. Leonard's Pl.
Museum Gardens
Municipal Offices
Central Library
Duncombe Pl.
St. Michael-le-Belfry Ch.
Salmery Ter.
Earlsborough Ter.
Frederic Street
Hetherton St.
The Esplanade
Hospitium
Multangular Tower
Tower
St. Leonard's Hospital
Twelfth Century House
Cinder Lane
The Astronomical Observatory
Assembly Rooms
Judge's Lodgings
Blake St.
Stonegate
National Railway Museum
Lendal Tower
Museum St.
Lendal
St. Helen's Church
G.P.O. Sorting Office
War Memorial Gardens
York City Rowing Club
G.P.O.
St. Helen's Sq.
Davygate
Leeman Road
Lendal Bridge
Municipal Offices
Mansion House
Coney
Station Rise
Station Ave.
Guildhall
New St.
St Martin-le-Grand Church
Tanners Moat
Wellington Row
Station Road
Rougier St.
Tanner St.
Row
Riverside Walk
River
British Rail H.Q. (Eastern Region)
All Saints Lane
North Street
York Railway Station
Rail Riders World
All Saints Church
St. Michael Ch.
Tanner Row
George Hudson St.
Station Road
Toft Green
Barker Lane
P.O.
Arts Centre
Micklegate
Bridge St.
Ouse Bridge
St. Martin's Lane
St. Martin-cum-Gregory Church
Trinity Lane
Queen's Staith Road
Queen's Staith
Holy Trinity Church
Fetter Lane
Bar La.
Sports and Community Centre
Bishophill
Buckingham St.
Priory Street
St. Mary's Church
Skeldergate
Queen St.
Micklegate Bar
Dewsbury Cotts.
Bishophill Junior
Smales St.
Prospect Ter.
Queens Staith Mews Lane
Dewsbury Ter.
Senior St.
Carr's Lane
Fairfax St.
Blossom St.
The Bar Convent Mus.
Nunnery La.
Lower Priory St.
Hampden St.
Cromwell
Lowther Ter.
The Crescent
Odeon Cinema
Victor Street
Kyme Street
Falkland St.
Baile Hill
P.O.
South Parade
Moss Street
Scarcroft Lane
Victoria Bar
Newton Terrace
The Mount
Shaw's Terrace
Dale Street
St.
Baile Hill Ter.
East Mount Road
Swann St.
Custance Walk
St. Benedict Rd.
Park St.

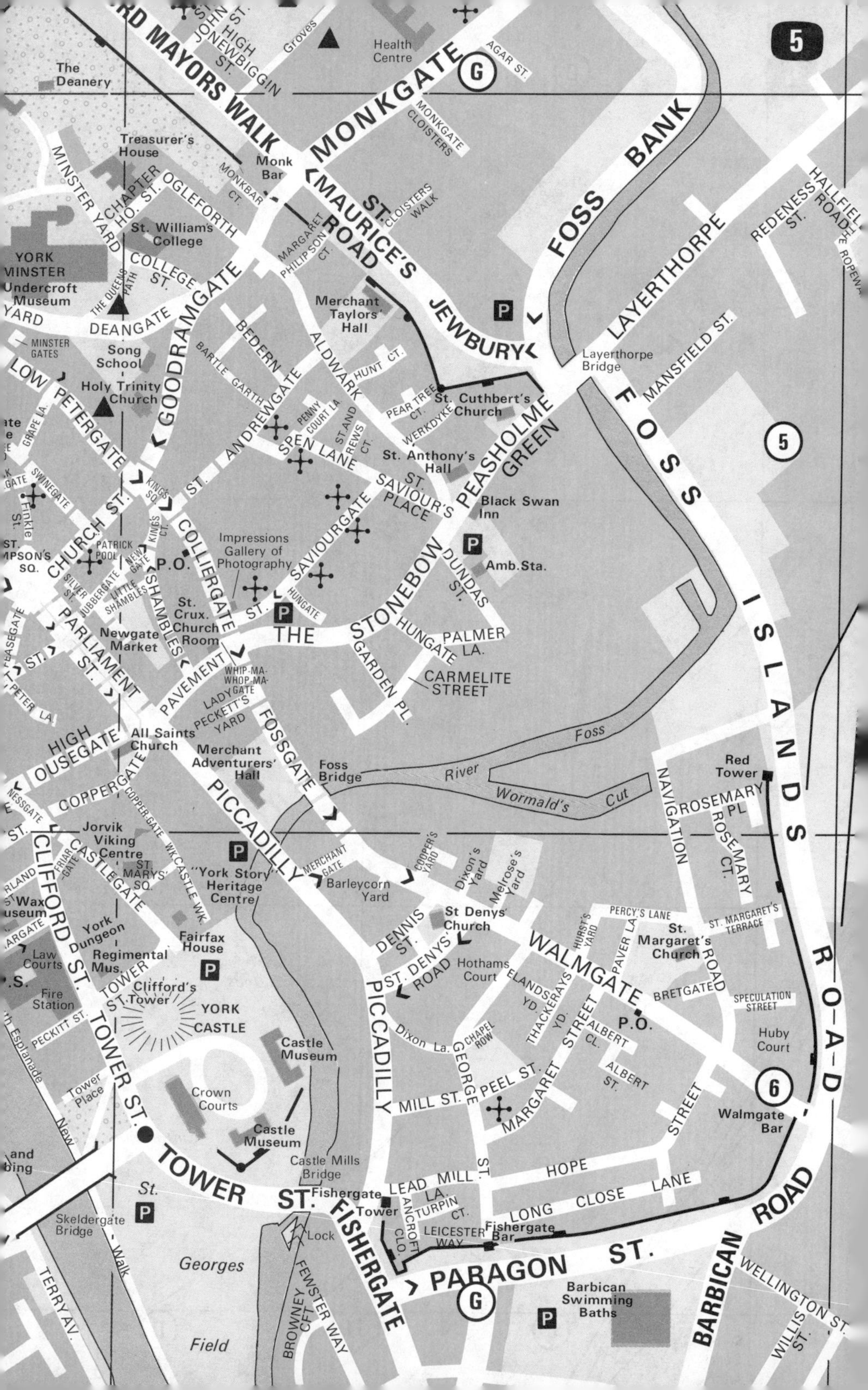
LORD MAYORS WALK
ST. JOHN ST.
HIGH NEWBIGGIN ST.
Groves
Health Centre
MONKGATE
AGAR ST.
The Deanery
MONKGATE CLOISTERS
Treasurer's House
MINSTER YARD
CHAPTER HO. ST.
OGLEFORTH
Monk Bar
MONKBAR CT.
ST. MAURICE'S ROAD
CLOISTERS WALK
FOSS BANK
HALLFIELD ROAD
REDENESS ST.
ROPEWALK
St. William's College
YORK MINSTER
Undercroft Museum
COLLEGE ST.
THE QUEENS PATH
MARGARET PHILIPSON CT.
LAYERTHORPE
YARD
DEANGATE
Merchant Taylors' Hall
JEWBURY
MINSTER GATES
Song School
GOODRAMGATE
BEDERN
BARTLE GARTH
ALDWARK
HUNT CT.
Layerthorpe Bridge
MANSFIELD ST.
LOW PETERGATE
Holy Trinity Church
ANDREWGATE
PENNY COURT LA.
ST. ANDREWS CT.
PEAR TREE CT.
St. Cuthbert's Church
WERKDYKE
PEASHOLME GREEN
FOSS ISLANDS ROAD
5
GRAPE LA.
SWINEGATE
SPEN LANE
St. Anthony's Hall
ST. SAVIOUR'S PLACE
Finkle St.
CHURCH ST.
KINGS SQ.
KINGS CT.
ST. ANDREWGATE
SAVIOURGATE
Black Swan Inn
ST. SAMPSON'S SQ.
PATRICK POOL
NEW GATE
P.O.
COLLIERGATE
Impressions Gallery of Photography
Amb. Sta.
DUNDAS ST.
SILVER ST.
JUBBERGATE
LITTLE SHAMBLES
SHAMBLES
St. Crux. Church Room
ST. HUNGATE
THE STONEBOW
HUNGATE
PALMER LA.
PARLIAMENT ST.
Newgate Market
PAVEMENT
WHIP-MA-WHOP-MA-GATE
GARDEN PL.
CARMELITE STREET
PEASEGATE
ST. PETER LA.
LADY PECKETT'S YARD
FOSSGATE
Foss
HIGH OUSEGATE
All Saints Church
Merchant Adventurers' Hall
Foss Bridge
River
Wormald's Cut
Red Tower
NESSGATE
COPPERGATE
COPPER-GATE WK.
PICCADILLY
NAVIGATION ROAD
ROSEMARY PL.
ROSEMARY CT.
ST.
CLIFFORD ST.
Jorvik Viking Centre
FRIARGATE
CASTLEGATE
ST. MARYS' SQ.
CASTLE WK.
"York Story" Heritage Centre
MERCHANT GATE
Barleycorn Yard
COOPER'S YARD
Dixon's Yard
Melrose's Yard
Wax Museum
Law Courts
York Dungeon
Regimental Mus.
Fairfax House
DENNIS ST.
St Denys' Church
PERCY'S LANE
HURST'S YARD
PAVER LA.
St. Margaret's Church
ST. MARGARET'S TERRACE
WALMGATE
ST. DENYS' ROAD
Hothams Court
ELANDS YD.
THACKERAYS YD.
BRETGATE
SPECULATION STREET
Fire Station
TOWER ST.
Clifford's Tower
YORK CASTLE
P.O.
Huby Court
PECKITT ST.
Dixon La.
CHAPEL ROW
GEORGE ST.
ALBERT CL.
ALBERT ST.
MARGARET STREET
Castle Museum
6
New Esplanade
Tower Place
Crown Courts
PEEL ST.
MILL ST.
STREET
Walmgate Bar
Castle Museum
Castle Mills Bridge
HOPE
LEAD MILL LA.
LONG CLOSE LANE
TOWER ST.
St.
Fishergate Tower
FISHERGATE
TURPIN CT.
ANCROFT CLO.
LEICESTER WAY
Fishergate Bar
PARAGON ST.
BARBICAN ROAD
Skeldergate Bridge
Lock
Walk
Georges
Field
TERRY AV.
FEWSTER WAY
BROWNEY CFT.
G
Barbican Swimming Baths
WELLINGTON ST.
WILLIS ST.
P

6

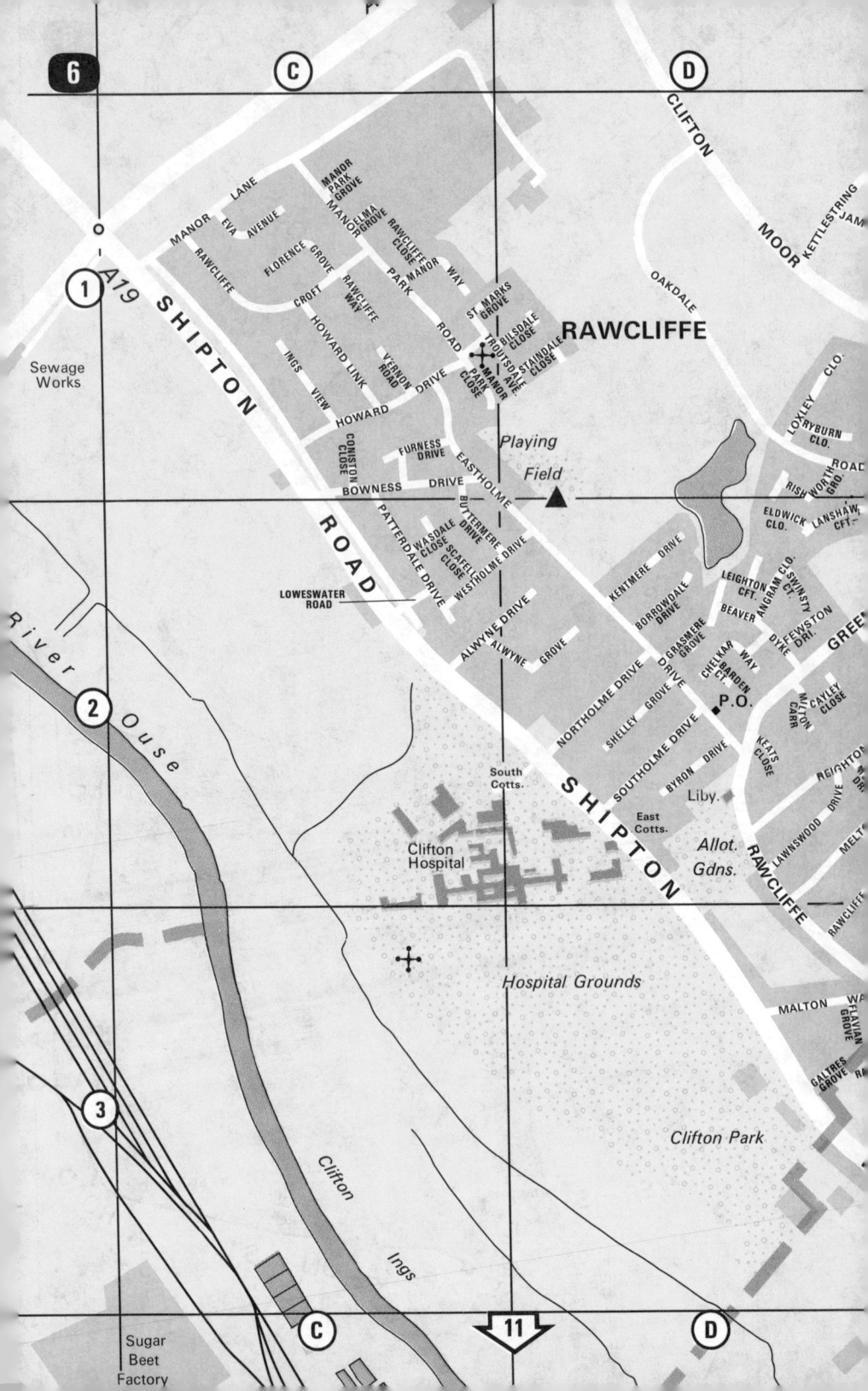

RAWCLIFFE

- Manor Lane
- Manor Park Grove
- Eva Avenue
- Manor Park Grove
- Rawcliffe Close
- Manor Grove
- Alma Grove
- Florence Grove
- Manor Way
- Croft
- Rawcliffe Way
- Park
- Manor Road
- St Marks Grove
- Bilsdale Close
- Oakdale
- Howard Link
- Vernon Drive
- Routsdale
- Staindale Close
- Clifton Moor
- Kettlestring
- Ings View
- Howard
- Manor Park Close
- Loxley Clo.
- Loxyburn Clo.
- Coniston Close
- Furness Drive
- Eastholme Drive
- Rishworth Gro.
- Bowness Drive
- Buttermere Drive
- Playing Field
- Eldwick Clo.
- Lanshaw Cft.
- Patterdale Drive
- Wasdale Close
- Scafell Close
- Westholme Drive
- Leighton Cft.
- Angram Clo.
- Swinsty Cft.
- Loweswater Road
- Alwyne Drive
- Alwyne Grove
- Kentmere Drive
- Borrowdale Drive
- Beaver Dyke Dri.
- Fewston Way
- Grasmere Grove
- Chelkar Way
- Barden Ct.
- Milton Carr
- Cayley Close
- Northolme Drive
- Shelley Grove
- Southolme Drive
- Byron Drive
- Keats Close
- Leighton
- P.O.
- South Cotts.
- East Cotts.
- Liby.
- Allot. Gdns.
- Lawnswood Drive
- Melt...
- Clifton Hospital
- Shipton Road
- Rawcliffe
- Hospital Grounds
- Malton Way
- Flavian Grove
- Gaitres Grove
- Clifton Park
- Clifton Ings
- River Ouse
- A19
- Sewage Works
- Sugar Beet Factory

① A19
② River Ouse
③
⑪

Driving Range
E
F
7
LA.
WATER LANE
GEORGE CAYLEY DRI.
HOLSON LINK
B1363
1
BRANSHOLME DR.
LANE
WATER LANE
BOWLAND WAY
HASTINGS CLO.
HARROW GLADE WAY
LANCASTER
HENDON GARTH
HALIFAX CT.
GARLANDS
ORIEL GRO.
GREEN CLOSE
DRIVE
SAVILLE GROVE
AVENUE
WIGGINTON
Playing Fields
2
8
SUTTON WAY
LITTLE AVE.
KINGSWAY NORTH
KINGSWAY NORTH
WAVENEY GR.
ASHTON AVENUE
INGRAM AVE.
BURTON STONE LANE
AVENUE
AVENUE
Chocolate Factory
AVE.
BUR DIKE
P.O.
LINK AVE.
BURRILL AVE.
CRICHTON
LUCAS
ROWNTREE
ROAD
Playing Fields
FAIRWAY
ST. PETER HILL DRIVE
AVENUE
NORTH
NORTH
ST. PHILIP'S GROVE
Playing Fields
SPALDING
KINGSWAY
KINGSWAY
AVENUE
EVELYN CRES.
AVENUE
BEDE AVE.
INTAKE AVE.
AVENUE
Freigh
HAMBLETON TERRA
3
WATER
CROMBIE
HORNER
STREET
TENNYSON AVENUE
ROAD
VIEW
STRE
CROMER
WILBERFORCE
GARTH TER.
FIELD
HAUGHTON
ALLAN ST.
MURROUGH WILSON PLACE
NEWBY TER.
WIGGINTON TER.
BELGRAVE ST.
CLARENDON ST.
BROMPTON ROAD
LISTER WAY
LANE
WHARTON AVE.
SURTEES ST.
LANE
RATCLIFFE
HILLSBOROUGH TERRACE
FEVERSHAM CRESCENT
CLARENDON COURT
HUDSON CRESCENT
LADY ROAD
STREET
STREET
VYNER ST.
Health Centre
Playing Fields
BURTON AVE.
GLENCOE
FALSGRAVE CRESCENT
STREET
UPPER NEWBOROUGH ST.
TER.
FOUNTAYNE ST.
OUSE LEA
CLIFTON PLACE
GUARDIAN COURT
BACK WEST VW.
ST.
PEMBROKE ST.
BAKER ST.
BRIGG'S ST.
SCAIFE ST.
SCAIFE GDNS.
PINFOLD CT.
STREET
ST. LUKE'S GROVE
STONE
SHIPTON
HUDSON ST.
FILEY TER.
York District Hospital
York Rugby League F.C.
LUMLEY
ABBEY STREET
STREET
12
York City A.F.C.
E
F
END
CLIFTON GREEN
HIGHCLIFFE COURT
AVENUE ROAD
P.O.
NEWBOROUGH
Footbridge
Clarence Gardens

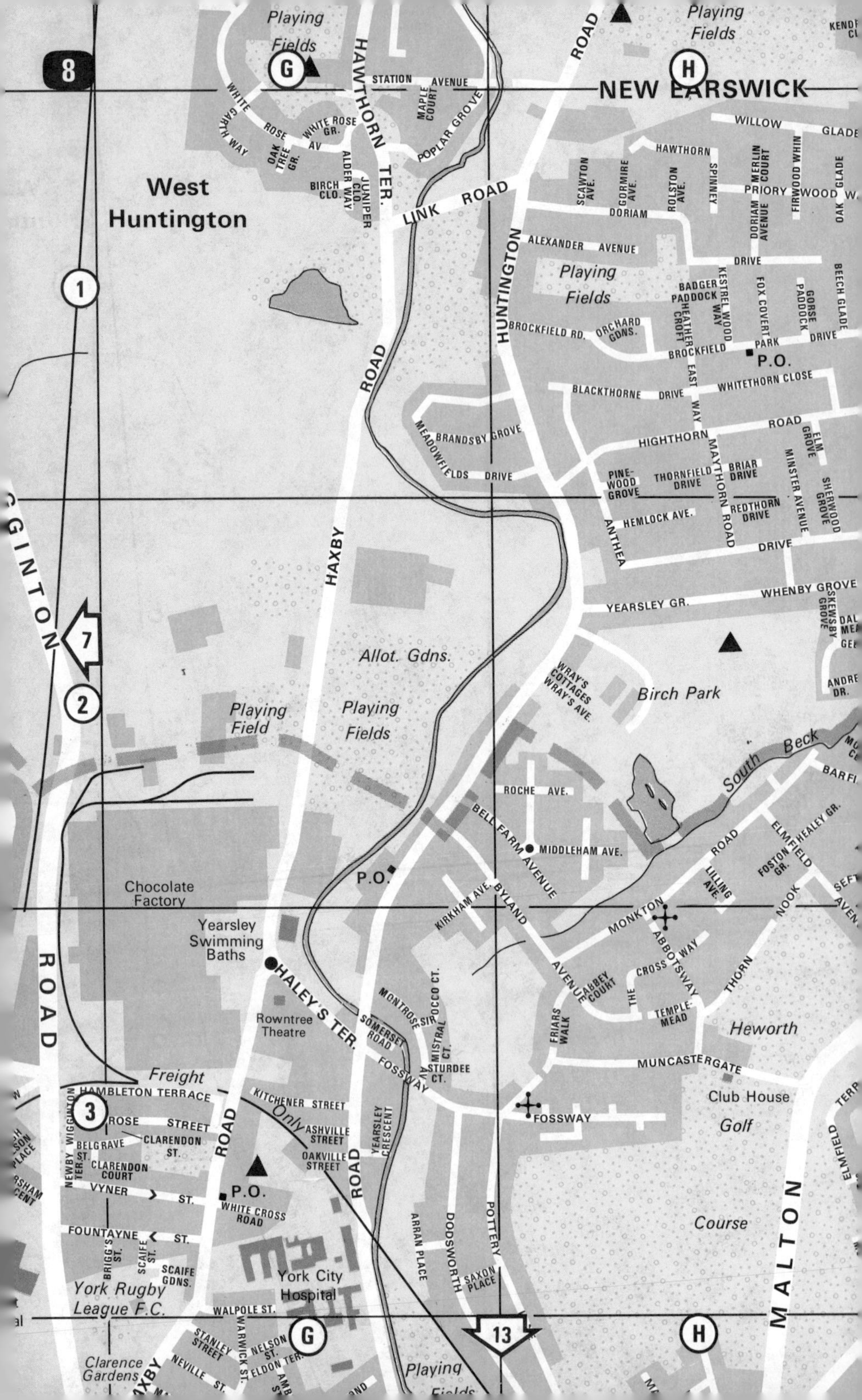

8
Playing Fields
G
H
NEW EARSWICK
HAWTHORN TER.
STATION AVENUE
MAPLE COURT
POPLAR GROVE
WHITE GARTH WAY
WHITE ROSE AV
WHITE ROSE GR.
OAK TREE GR.
ALDER WAY
JUNIPER CLO.
BIRCH CLO.
LINK ROAD
West Huntington
HUNTINGTON ROAD
WILLOW GLADE
HAWTHORN SPINNEY
SCAWTON AVE.
GORMIRE AVE.
ROLSTON AVE.
MERLIN COURT
FIRWOOD WHIN
PRIORY WOOD W.
OAK GLADE
DORIAM AVENUE
DORIAM DRIVE
ALEXANDER AVENUE
Playing Fields
BADGER PADDOCK
KESTREL WOOD WAY
HEATHER CROFT
FOX COVERT
GORSE PADDOCK
BEECH GLADE
BROCKFIELD RD.
ORCHARD GDNS.
BROCKFIELD PARK DRIVE
P.O.
BLACKTHORNE DRIVE
WHITETHORN CLOSE
EAST WAY
HIGHTHORN ROAD
ELM GROVE
BRANDSBY GROVE
MEADOWFIELDS DRIVE
PINEWOOD GROVE
THORNFIELD DRIVE
BRIAR DRIVE
MAYTHORN ROAD
MINSTER AVENUE
SHERWOOD GROVE
HEMLOCK AVE.
REDTHORN DRIVE
ANTHEA DRIVE
YEARSLEY GR.
WHENBY GROVE
SKEWSBY GROVE
HAXBY ROAD
GINTON ROAD
7
1
2
Allot. Gdns.
Playing Field
Playing Fields
WRAY'S COTTAGES
WRAY'S AVE.
Birch Park
ANDREW DR.
South Beck
BARFIELD
ROCHE AVE.
BELL FARM AVENUE
MIDDLEHAM AVE.
HEALEY GR.
ELMFIELD
FOSTON GR.
LILLING AVE.
MONKTON ROAD
NOOK
Chocolate Factory
Yearsley Swimming Baths
HALEY'S TER.
KIRKHAM AVE.
BYLAND AVENUE
ABBOTSWAY
THE CROSS WAY
THORN
ABBEY COURT
TEMPLEMEAD
FRIARS WALK
Heworth
MONTROSE
ROCCO CT.
SIR MISTRAL CT.
SOMERSET ROAD
Rowntree Theatre
FOSSWAY
STURDEE CT.
MUNCASTERGATE
Club House
Golf Course
Freight Only
HAMBLETON TERRACE
3
ROSE STREET
CLARENDON ST.
CLARENDON COURT
BELGRAVE ST.
NEWBY TER.
WIGGINTON
KITCHENER STREET
ASHVILLE STREET
OAKVILLE STREET
YEARSLEY CRESCENT
FOSSWAY
VYNER ST.
P.O.
WHITE CROSS ROAD
FOUNTAYNE ST.
BRIGG'S ST.
SCAIFE ST.
SCAIFE GDNS.
York Rugby League F.C.
York City Hospital
ARRAN PLACE
DODSWORTH
POTTERY
SAXON PLACE
MALTON
ELMFIELD TERR.
WALPOLE ST.
STANLEY STREET
WARWICK ST.
NELSON ST.
ELDON TER.
NEVILLE ST.
Clarence Gardens
13
Playing Fields

9

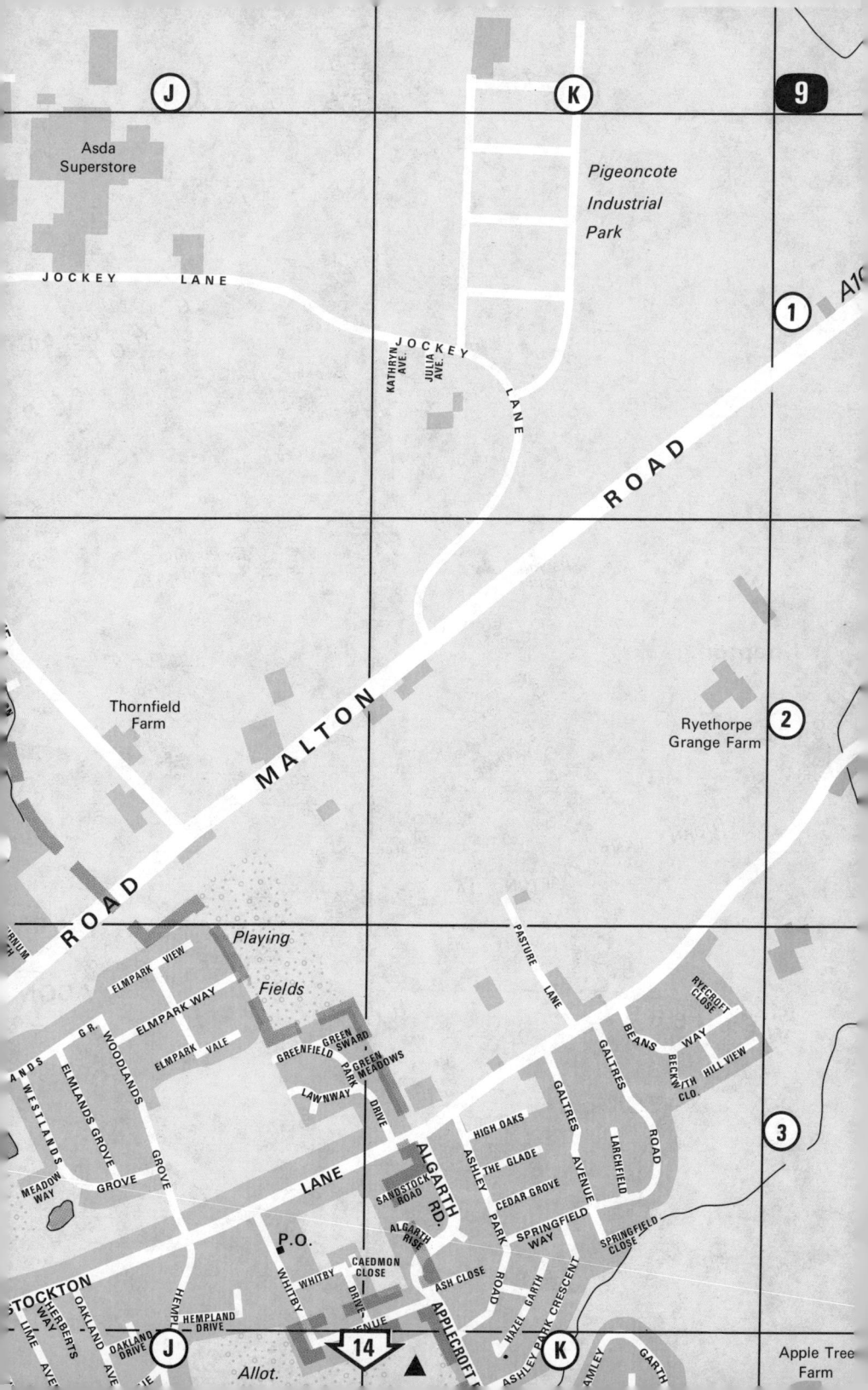

J **K**

Asda Superstore

Pigeoncote Industrial Park

JOCKEY LANE

KATHRYN AVE.
JULIA AVE.
JOCKEY LANE

A10

①

MALTON ROAD

Thornfield Farm

Ryethorpe Grange Farm

②

ROAD

Playing Fields

PASTURE LANE

RYECROFT CLOSE

ELMPARK VIEW
GR. WOODLANDS
ELMPARK WAY
ELMPARK VALE
GREENFIELD
GREEN SWARD
GREEN MEADOWS
LAWNWAY
PARK DRIVE
BEANS WAY
BECKWITH CLO.
HILL VIEW
GALTRES
GALTRES AVENUE
LARCHFIELD
ROAD

ELMLANDS GROVE
WESTLANDS GROVE
MEADOW WAY
LANE
ALGARTH RD.
SANDSTOCK ROAD
ALGARTH RISE
HIGH OAKS
THE GLADE
ASHLEY PARK
CEDAR GROVE
SPRINGFIELD WAY
SPRINGFIELD CLOSE

③

P.O.
WHITBY DRIVE
CAEDMON CLOSE
ASH CLOSE
HAZEL GARTH
ASHLEY PARK CRESCENT

STOCKTON
HERBERTS WAY
OAKLAND AVE.
OAKLAND DRIVE
LIME AVENUE
HEMPLAND DRIVE
WHITBY AVENUE
14
APPLECROFT
AMLEY GARTH

Apple Tree Farm

J **K**

Allot.

A
B
A59
WESTVIEW CLOSE
LOW POPPLETON LANE
Playing Field
TRENCHARD ROAD
PORTAL ROAD
MILL GATES
LANGHOLME DRIVE
THE PADDOCK
FARFIELD
PLANTATION DRIVE
NEWLANDS DRIVE
GROVE
PADDOCK WAY
BOROUGHBR
P.O.
PLANTATI GROVE
LIDGETT GROVE
AVENUE
SHERWOOD GROVE
ALBION AVENUE
NORMAN DRIVE
LANE
WHEATLANDS
SHIRLEY
OUSEBURN
AVENUE
CRANBROOK
MELWOOD GROVE
GRAYSHON DRIVE
ALMSFORD DRIVE
ALMSFORD
SITWELL GROVE
CRANBROOK AVE
GARBU
MELWOOD GROVE
CELTIC CLOSE
JORVIK CLO.
ROAD
P.O.
Playing Field
Playing Fields
OSTMAN ROAD
IVER CLOSE
4
Knapton
BACK LANE
GREENBOROUGH AV.
DRI.
JUTE ROAD
KENRICK PLACE
VIKING ROAD
SMEATON GROVE
TOSTIG AVENUE
Allot. Gdns.
DRIVE
WOODLEA GROVE
VILLAGE STREET
5
TURNBERRY
BIRKDALE GRO.
MUIRFIELD WAY
CARNOUSTIE CLO.
DANE
FAWKES DRIVE
DANEBURY
WOODLEA CRES.
LOWFIELD LANE
TEN THORN LANE
LOCH RIN PL.
MELANDER CLO.
COURCEY GROVE
MOWBRAY DRIVE
JUTE ROAD
WOODLEA AVENUE
WOODLEA BAN.
LANE
KNAPTON LANE
BECKFIELD LANE
BECKFIELD PL.
GRESLEY CT.
RAVEN GRO.
DANEBURY CRES.
DRIVE
BEECH AVENUE
STAITHES CLOSE
BLAND LANE
BRIAR AVE.
COLLINGHAM PL.
FELLBROOK AVENUE
RUNSWICK AVE.
DANEBURY
ROSEDALE
GRANGER AVENUE
GRANGER PL.
CHESTNUT GR.
GROVE
ACOM
B1224
WETHERBY ROAD
RIDGEWAY
CROFT SIDE
CROFT WAY
KIRK VIEW
YORK
CROSS ST
CHAPEL FIELDS ROAD
Chapel Fields
BRIDLE WAY
BRAMHAM GROVE
6
MARSTON CR.
MARSTON AVENUE
RIDGEWAY
THE GREEN
GROVE TER.
STREET
ACOMB MEWS
P.O.
BE GRE
BARKSTON
BRANTON PLACE
BRAMHAM AVENUE
ROAD
Rec. Grd.
Liby.
P
SOUTH VIEW TER.
RYLATT PLACE
FRONT
BARKSTON ROAD
AVENUE
HESSAY PLACE
BARKSTON GROVE
BARKSTON CLOSE
BRAMHAM
HAMMERTON CLOSE
WALTON PLACE
LANE
VESPER DRIVE
LOWFIELDS DRIVE
KIR CRESCENT
DIJON
AVENUE
CHAPEL FIELDS RD.
THE WANDLE
HOTHAM AVE
PARKER
A
LANE
16
VESPER DRI.
BACHELOR HILL
GALE
B
Playing F
Low Fiel

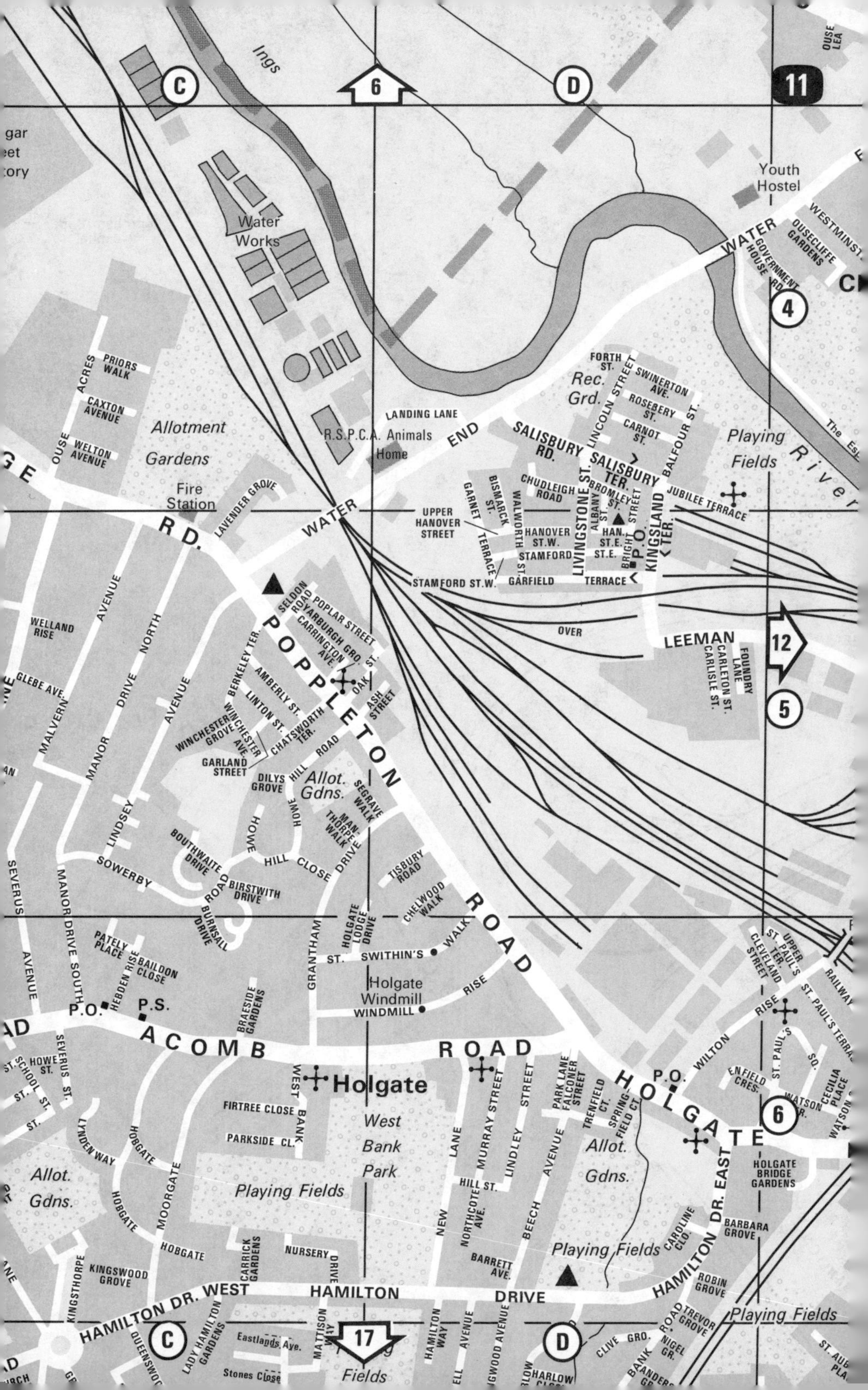
Ings
C
6
D
Ouse Lea
Youth Hostel
Water Works
WATER END
GOVERNMENT HOUSE RD.
OUSECLIFFE GARDENS
WESTMINSTER
4
FORTH ST.
SWINERTON AVE.
ROSEBERY ST.
CARNOT ST.
LINCOLN STREET
BALFOUR ST.
Rec. Grd.
PRIORS WALK
ACRES
CAXTON AVENUE
WELTON AVENUE
OUSE
Allotment Gardens
LANDING LANE
R.S.P.C.A. Animals Home
SALISBURY RD.
SALISBURY TER.
Playing Fields
River
CHUDLEIGH ROAD
BROMLEY ST.
Fire Station
LAVENDER GROVE
RD.
WATER
UPPER HANOVER STREET
GARNET TERRACE
BISMARCK ST.
WALWORTH ST.
LIVINGSTONE ST.
ALBANY ST.
STREET
BRIGHT
P.O.
KINGSLAND TER.
JUBILEE TERRACE
HANOVER ST.W.
HAN. ST.E.
STAMFORD ST.E.
GARFIELD
TERRACE
STAMFORD ST.W.
SELDON ROAD
POPLAR STREET
YARBURGH GRO.
CARRINGTON AVE
OAK ST.
ASH STREET
POPPLETON
OVER
LEEMAN
CARLETON ST.
CARLISLE ST.
FOUNDRY LANE
12
5
WELLAND RISE
AVENUE
NORTH
GLEBE AVE.
MALVERN
MANOR
DRIVE
BERKELEY TER.
AMBERLY ST.
LINTON ST.
CHATSWORTH TER.
WINCHESTER GROVE
WINCHESTER AVE
GARLAND STREET
DILYS GROVE
HILL
ROAD
Allot. Gdns.
SEGRAVE WALK
MANTHORPE WALK
HOWE
LINDSEY
BOUTHWAITE DRIVE
SOWERBY
SEVERUS
MANOR DRIVE SOUTH
CLOSE
DRIVE
TISBURY ROAD
CHELWOOD WALK
BIRSTWITH DRIVE
BURNSALL DRIVE
HOLGATE LODGE DRIVE
GRANTHAM
ST. SWITHIN'S WALK
ROAD
PATELY PLACE
HEBDEN RISE
BAILDON CLOSE
BRAESIDE GARDENS
Holgate Windmill
RISE
WINDMILL
P.O.
P.S.
ACOMB
ROAD
ST. PAUL'S TER.
UPPER ST. PAUL'S TER.
CLEVELAND STREET
RAILWAY
ST. PAUL'S TERRACE
WILTON RISE
ST. PAUL'S SQ.
ENFIELD CRES.
WATSON TER.
CECILIA PLACE
WATSON
HOWE ST.
SCHOOL ST.
SEVERUS ST.
WEST BANK
Holgate
MURRAY STREET
STREET
PARK LANE
FALCONER STREET
TRENFIELD CT.
SPRING FIELD CT.
HOLGATE
6
FIRTREE CLOSE
PARKSIDE CL.
West Bank Park
LANE
LINDLEY
AVENUE
Allot. Gdns.
HOLGATE BRIDGE GARDENS
LYNDEN WAY
HOBGATE
MOORGATE
Playing Fields
HILL ST.
NEW
NORTHCOTE AVE.
BEECH
HAMILTON DR. EAST
CAROLINE CLO.
BARBARA GROVE
Allot. Gdns.
HOBGATE
KINGSWOOD GROVE
CARRICK GARDENS
NURSERY DRIVE
BARRETT AVE.
Playing Fields
ROBIN GROVE
KINGSTHORPE
HAMILTON DR. WEST
HAMILTON
DRIVE
HAMILTON
TREVOR GROVE
ROAD
Playing Fields
LADY HAMILTON GARDENS
Eastlands Ave.
MATTISON WAY
17
HAMILTON WAY
AVENUE
D
CLIVE GRO.
NIGEL GR.
Stones Close
Fields
HARLOW
BANK
ST. AUBYNS PLACE

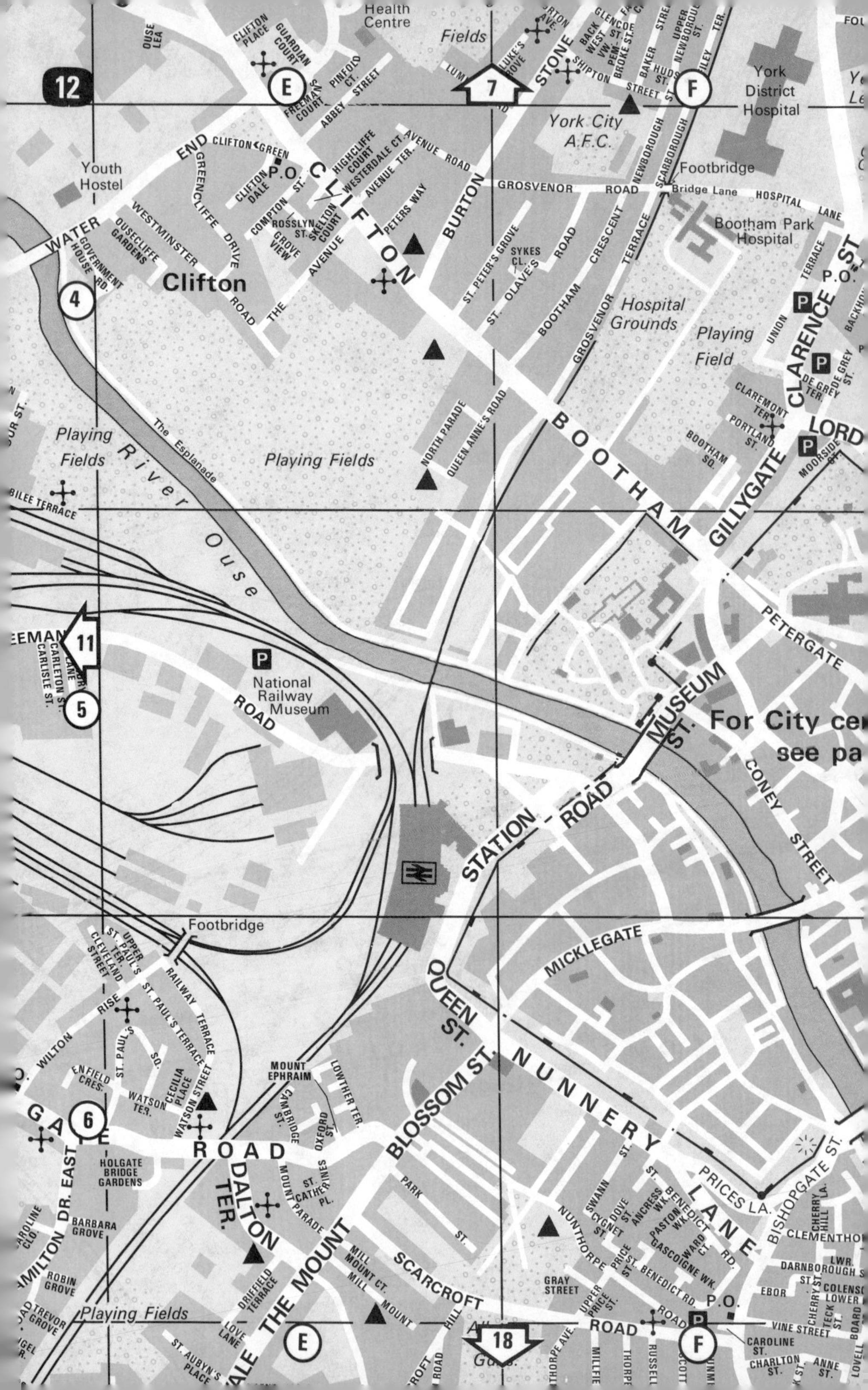
Health Centre
Fields
7
E
F
York District Hospital
York City A.F.C.
Youth Hostel
P.O.
CLIFTON
Clifton
WATER END
CLIFTON GREEN
GREENCLIFFE DRIVE
WESTMINSTER ROAD
OUSECLIFFE GARDENS
GOVERNMENT HOUSE RD.
CLIFTON PLACE
GUARDIAN COURT
FREEMAN'S COURT
PINFOLD CT.
ABBEY STREET
HIGHCLIFFE COURT
WESTERDALE CT.
AVENUE TER.
AVENUE ROAD
CLIFTON DALE
COMPTON ST.
ROSSLYN ST.
GROVE VIEW
SKELTON COURT
THE AVENUE
PETERS WAY
BURTON STONE
SHIPTON STREET
BAKER ST.
HUDS ST.
GROSVENOR ROAD
GROSVENOR TERRACE
NEWBOROUGH ST.
SCARBOROUGH
Footbridge
Bridge Lane
HOSPITAL LANE
Bootham Park Hospital
BOOTHAM CRESCENT
ST. OLAVE'S ROAD
SYKES CL.
ST. PETER'S GROVE
Hospital Grounds
Playing Field
Playing Fields
CLARENCE ST.
UNION TERRACE
DE GREY TER.
DE GREY ST.
CLAREMONT TER.
PORTLAND ST.
BOOTHAM SQ.
LORD
MOORSIDE
GILLYGATE
BOOTHAM
NORTH PARADE
QUEEN ANNE'S ROAD
The Esplanade
River Ouse
BILEE TERRACE
PETERGATE
MUSEUM ST.
For City centre see pa
11
CARLETON ST.
CARLISLE ST.
5
4
National Railway Museum
ROAD
STATION ROAD
CONEY STREET
Footbridge
MICKLEGATE
QUEEN ST.
BLOSSOM ST.
NUNNERY LANE
PRICES LA.
BISHOPGATE ST.
CHERRY HILL LA.
CLEMENTHORPE
DARNBOROUGH ST.
COLENSO ST.
EBOR
LOWER
UPPER ST. PAUL'S TER.
CLEVELAND STREET
RAILWAY TERRACE
ST. PAUL'S TERRACE
ST. PAUL'S SQ.
WILTON RISE
ENFIELD CRES.
WATSON TER.
CECILIA PLACE
WATSON STREET
MOUNT EPHRAIM
LOWTHER TER.
CAMBRIDGE ST.
OXFORD ST.
6
ROAD
HOLGATE BRIDGE GARDENS
DALTON TER.
ST. CATHERINES PL.
MOUNT PARADE
PARK ST.
THE MOUNT
MILL MOUNT CT.
MILL MOUNT
SCARCROFT ROAD
SCARCROFT HILL
NUNTHORPE ROAD
SWANN ST.
DOVE ST.
CYGNET ST.
ANCRESS WK.
ST. BENEDICT RD.
PASTON WK.
GASCOIGNE WK.
WARD CT.
PRICE ST.
UPPER PRICE ST.
GRAY STREET
BARBARA GROVE
HAMILTON DR. EAST
CAROLINE CLO.
ROBIN GROVE
TREVOR GROVE
Playing Fields
DRIFFIELD TERRACE
LOVE LANE
ST. AUBYN'S PLACE
18
VINE STREET
CAROLINE ST.
CHARLTON ST.
ANNE ST.
CHERRY ST.
TECK ST.
THORPE ST.
RUSSELL
P.O.

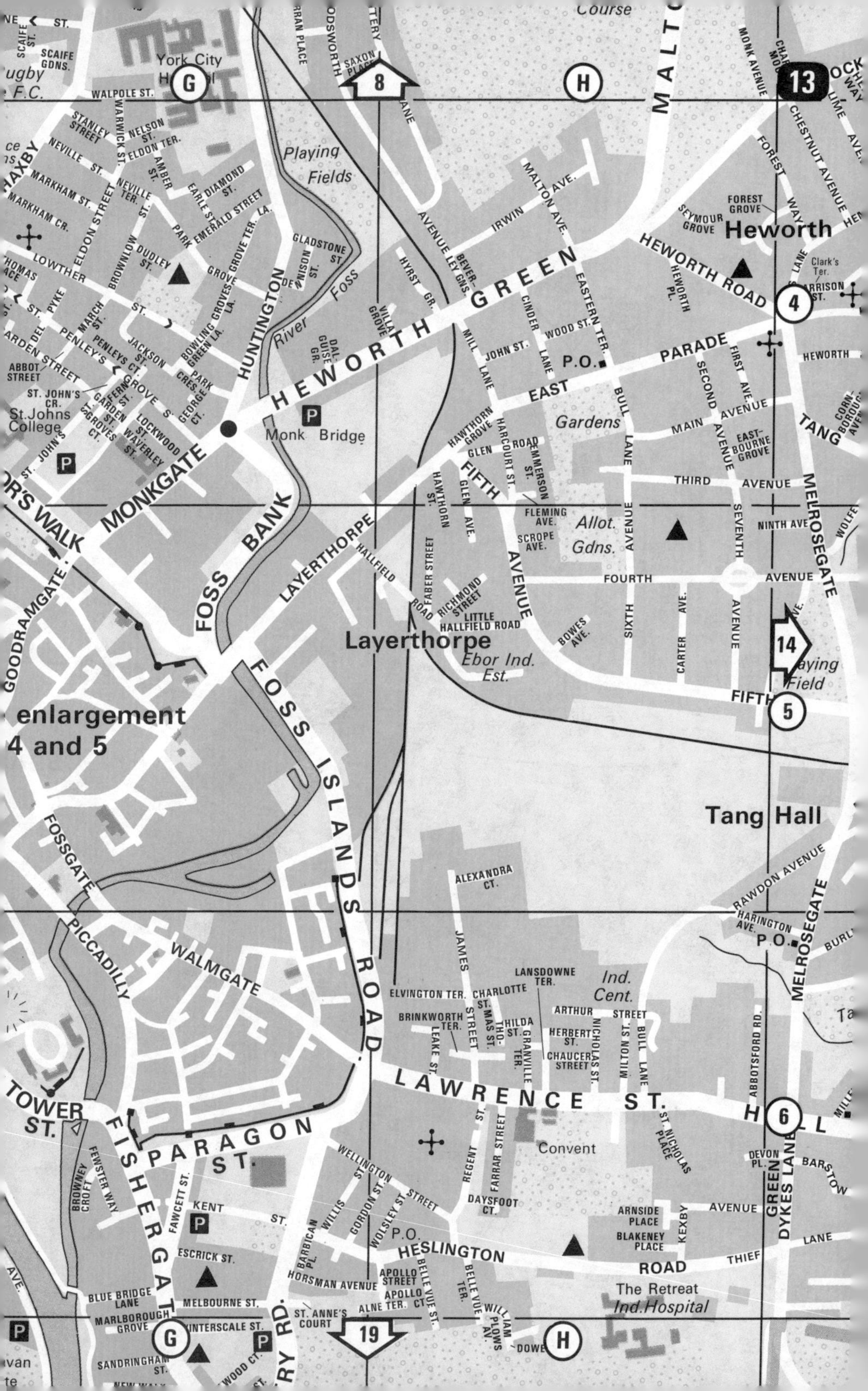

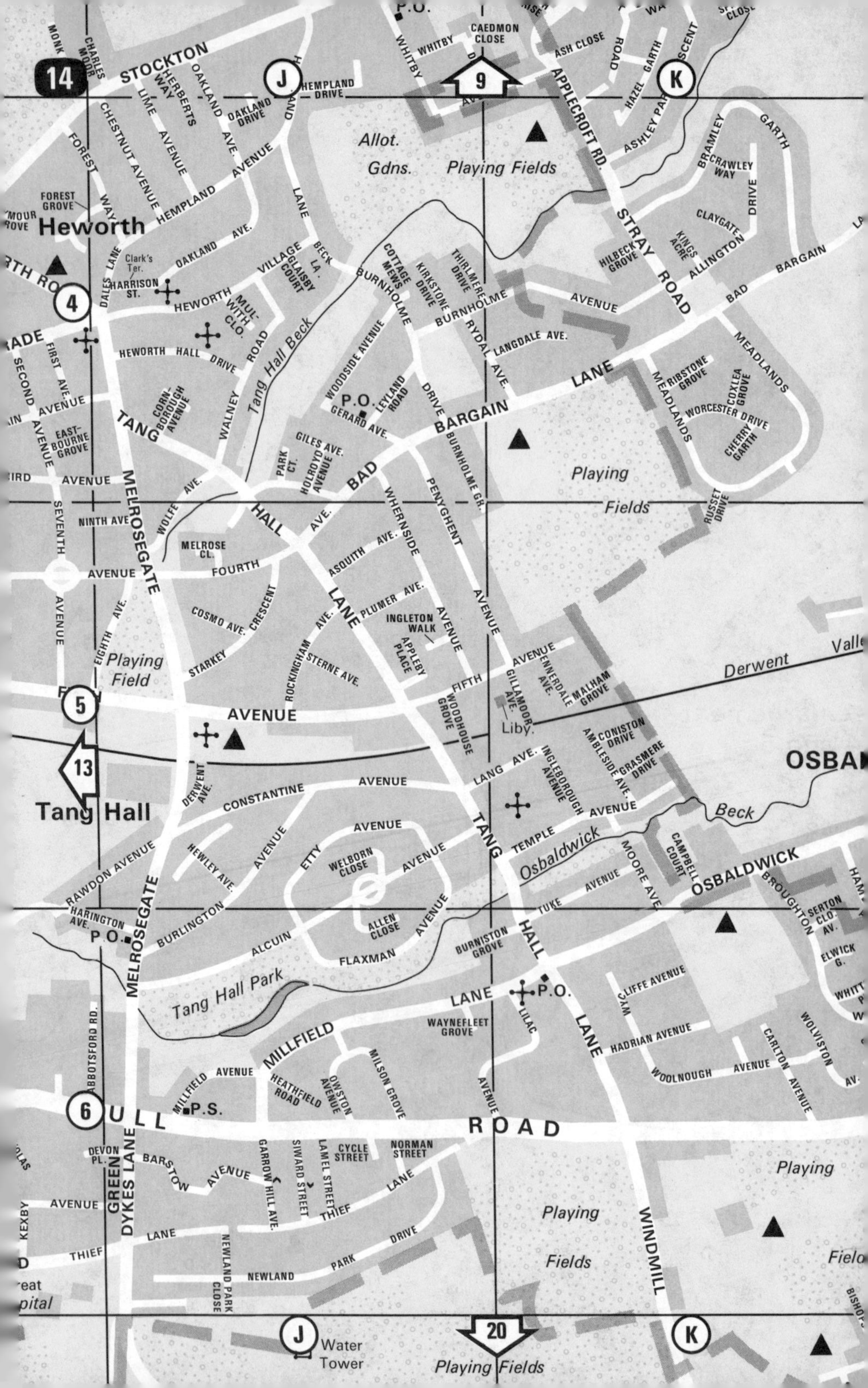
STOCKTON
CHARLES MOOR
MONK
HERBERTS WAY
LIME
CHESTNUT AVENUE
OAKLAND AVE.
OAKLAND DRIVE
HEMPLAND DRIVE
HEMPLAND AVENUE
FOREST WAY
FOREST GROVE
Heworth
Allot. Gdns.
Playing Fields
CAEDMON CLOSE
WHITBY
WHITBY AVE.
P.O.
9
ASH CLOSE
APPLECROFT RD.
HAZEL GARTH
ASHLEY PARK CRESCENT
BRAMLEY GARTH
CRAWLEY WAY
DRIVE
CLAYGATE
KINGS ACRE
ALLINGTON
STRAY ROAD
HILBECK GROVE
BAD BARGAIN LANE
AVENUE
BURNHOLME
BURNHOLME DRIVE
COTTAGE MEWS
KIRKSTONE DRIVE
THIRLMERE DRIVE
RYDAL AVE.
LANGDALE AVE.
MEADLANDS
RIBSTONE GROVE
COXLEA GROVE
WORCESTER DRIVE
CHERRY GARTH
RUSSET DRIVE
Playing Fields
VILLAGE
GLAISBY COURT
BECK LA.
Clark's Ter.
HARRISON ST.
HEWORTH
MUL-WITH CLO.
HEWORTH HALL DRIVE
ROAD
Tang Hall Beck
WALNEY
CORNBOROUGH AVENUE
WOODSIDE AVENUE
P.O.
LEYLAND ROAD
GERARD AVE.
GILES AVE.
HOLROYD AVENUE
PARK CT.
BURNHOLME GR.
PENYGHENT AVENUE
WHERNSIDE AVE.
ASQUITH AVE.
PLUMER AVE.
INGLETON WALK
APPLEBY PLACE
STERNE AVE.
ROCKINGHAM AVE.
FIRST AVE.
SECOND AVENUE
EASTBOURNE GROVE
SEVENTH AVENUE
NINTH AVE.
FOURTH AVENUE
EIGHTH AVE.
TANG HALL LANE
MELROSEGATE
WOLFE AVE.
MELROSE CL.
COSMO AVE.
CRESCENT
STARKEY
Playing Field
FIFTH AVENUE
WOODHOUSE GROVE
GILLAMOOR AVE.
Liby.
ENNERDALE AVE.
MALHAM GROVE
CONISTON DRIVE
AMBLESIDE AVE.
GRASMERE DRIVE
Derwent Valley
OSBA
5
13
Tang Hall
DERWENT AVE.
CONSTANTINE AVENUE
LANG AVE.
INGLEBOROUGH AVENUE
TEMPLE AVENUE
Beck
Osbaldwick
MOORE AVE.
CAMPBELL COURT
OSBALDWICK
BROUGHTON
SERTON CLO.
AV.
ELWICK G.
WHITT
HEWLEY AVE.
RAWDON AVENUE
ETTY AVENUE
WELBORN CLOSE
AVENUE
ALLEN CLOSE
HARINGTON AVE.
P.O.
BURLINGTON
ALCUIN
FLAXMAN
TUKE AVENUE
BURNISTON GROVE
CLIFFE AVENUE
Tang Hall Park
LANE
P.O.
LILAC
WAYNEFLEET GROVE
HADRIAN AVENUE
WOLVISTON
CARLTON AVENUE
WOOLNOUGH AVENUE
MILLFIELD
ABBOTSFORD RD.
MILLFIELD AVENUE
HEATHFIELD ROAD
OWSTON AVENUE
MILSON GROVE
AVENUE
P.S.
6
HULL ROAD
DEVON PL.
BARSTOW AVENUE
GARROW HILL AVE.
SIWARD STREET
LAMEL STREET
CYCLE STREET
NORMAN STREET
THIEF LANE
GREEN DYKES LANE
AVENUE
KEXBY
THIEF LANE
NEWLAND PARK DRIVE
NEWLAND PARK CLOSE
Playing Fields
WINDMILL
Playing Fields
Great Hospital
J
Water Tower
20
Playing Fields
K
BISHOP

Apple Tree
Farm

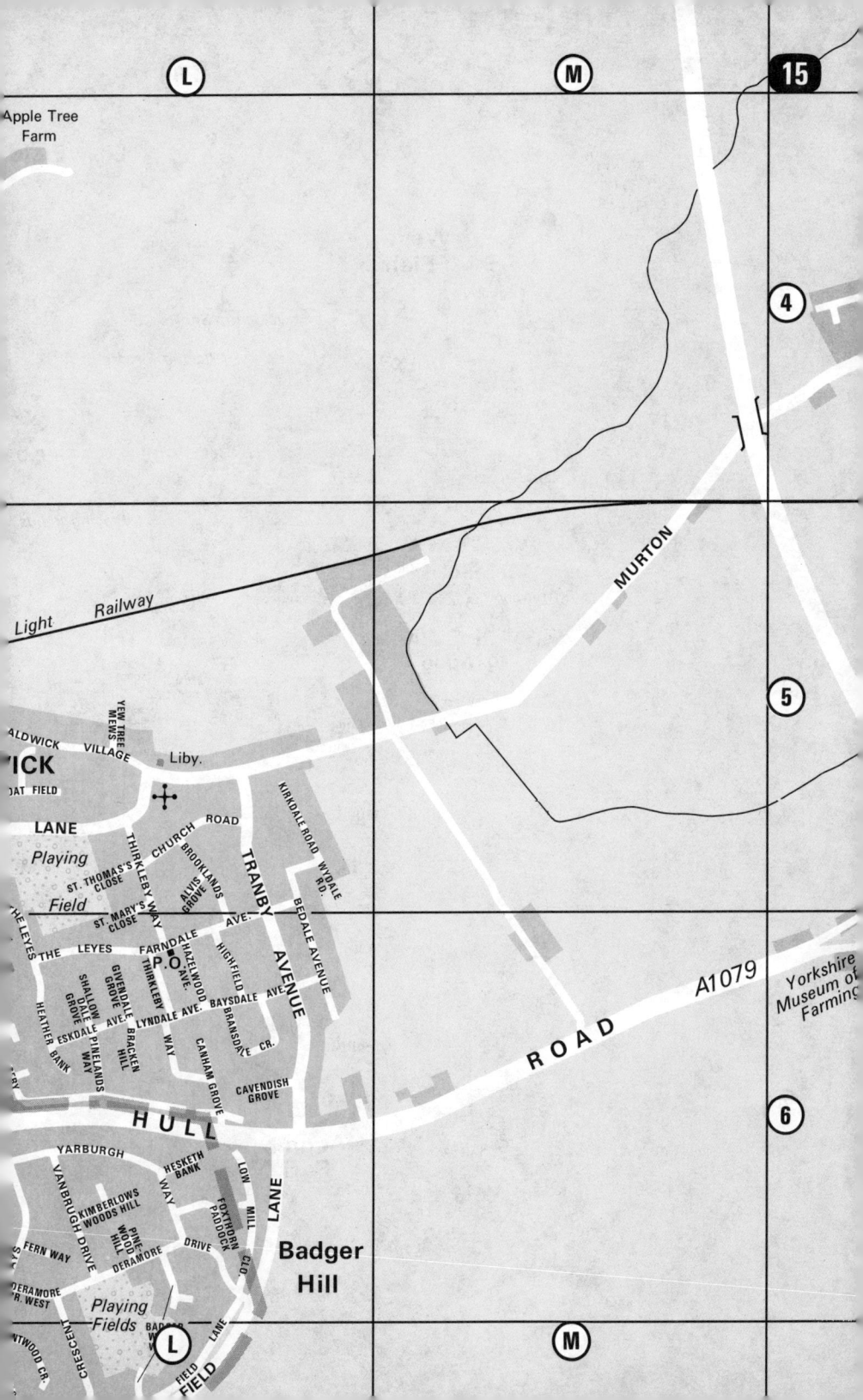

L M 15

4

5

Light Railway   MURTON

ALDWICK VILLAGE   YEW TREE MEWS   Liby.
ICK
OAT FIELD
LANE   CHURCH ROAD   KIRKDALE ROAD WYDALE
Playing   ST. THOMAS'S THIRKLEBY BROOKLANDS RD.
           CLOSE   WAY   ALVIS GROVE
Field   ST. MARY'S CLOSE   BEDALE AVENUE
                                                              TRANBY AVENUE
THE LEYES   FARNDALE P.O
            GROVE   HAZELWOOD   HIGHFIELD   A1079   Yorkshire
      SHALLOW GIVENDALE THIRKLEBY BAYSDALE AVE.   Museum of
      DALE   GROVE   WAY   ROAD   Farming
      GROVE   ESKDALE AVE. LYNDALE AVE. BRANSDALE
HEATHER BANK   PINELANDS   BRACKEN CR.
               WAY   HILL   CANHAM GROVE
                                   CAVENDISH GROVE
HULL
          YARBURGH   HESKETH BANK
     VANBRUGH DRIVE KIMBERLOWS LOW
                     WOODS HILL MILL
     FERN WAY   PINE FOXTHORN PADDOCK
                 WOOD CLO.
                 HILL DRIVE
     DERAMORE   DERAMORE   Badger
     CR. WEST   Hill
     Playing
     Fields   BADGER
CRESCENT   L   FIELD   LANE   M
              WOOD CR.   FIELD

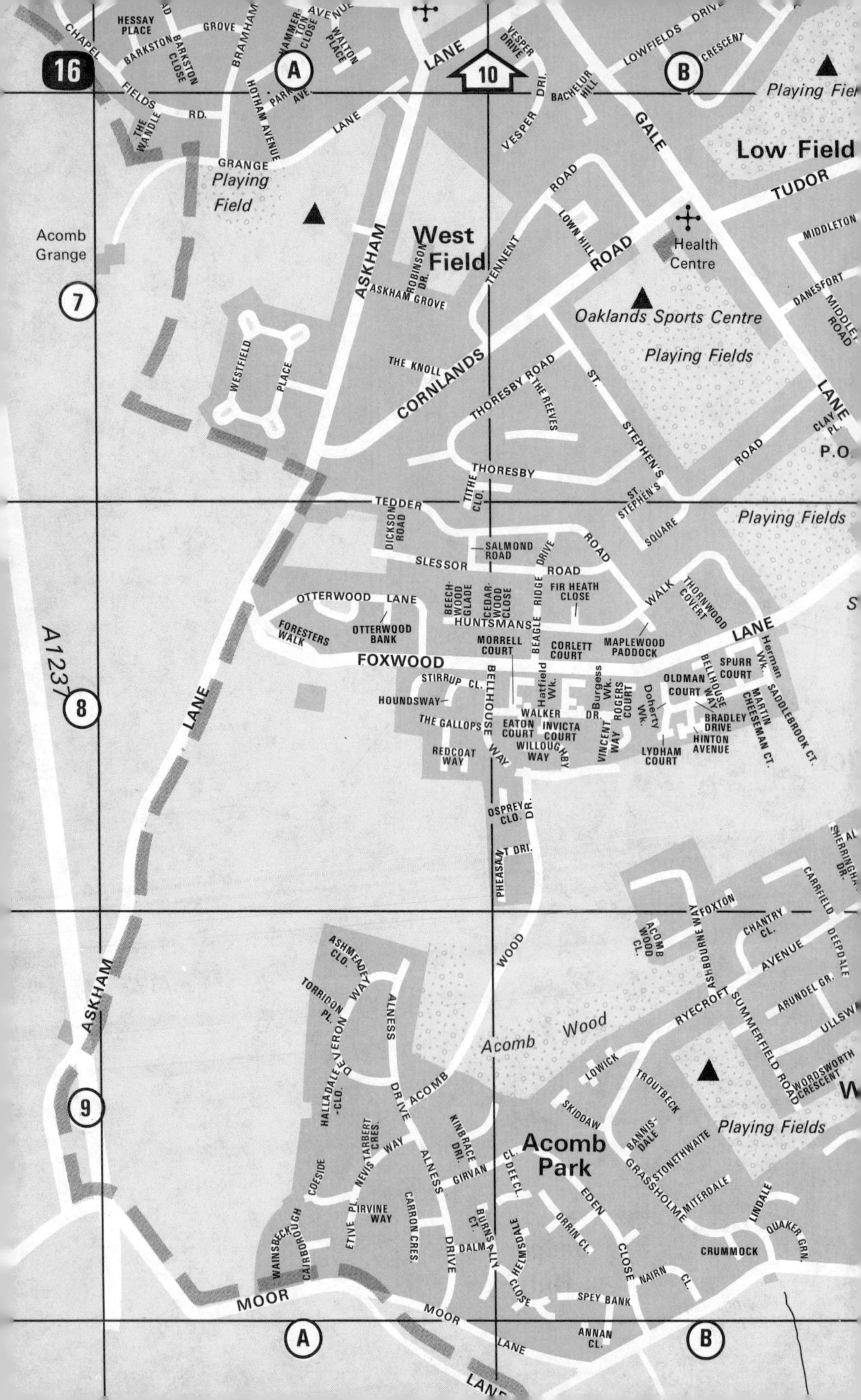

HESSAY PLACE
CHAPEL FIELDS RD.
GROVE
BARKSTON
BARKSTON CLOSE
BRAMHAM
HOTHAM AVENUE
HAMMERTON CLOSE
AVENUE
WALTON PLACE
PARK AVE.
THE WANDLE
GRANGE LANE
A
B
10
LANE
VESPER DRIVE
VESPER DRI.
BACHELOR HILL
LOWFIELDS DRIVE
CRESCENT
Playing Field
Playing Field
Low Field
GALE
TUDOR
MIDDLETON
Acomb Grange
7
ASKHAM
West Field
ROBINSON DR.
ASKHAM GROVE
TENNENT
ROAD
LOWN HILL
ROAD
Health Centre
DANESFORT
MIDDLETON ROAD
Oaklands Sports Centre
Playing Fields
WESTFIELD PLACE
THE KNOLL
CORNLANDS
THORESBY ROAD
THE REEVES
ST. STEPHEN'S
LANE
CLAY PL.
P.O.
ROAD
THORESBY
TITHE CLO.
TEDDER
ST. STEPHEN'S SQUARE
Playing Fields
DICKSON ROAD
SALMOND ROAD
SLESSOR
ROAD
RIDGE DRIVE
ROAD
FIR HEATH CLOSE
WALK
THORNWOOD COVERT
OTTERWOOD LANE
BEECHWOOD GLADE
CEDARWOOD CLOSE
BEAGLE
HUNTSMANS
FORESTERS WALK
OTTERWOOD BANK
MORRELL COURT
CORLETT COURT
MAPLEWOOD PADDOCK
LANE
A1237
FOXWOOD
STIRRUP CL.
BELLHOUSE
Hatfield Wk.
Burgess Wk.
ROGERS COURT
Doherty Wk.
OLDMAN COURT
BELLHOUSE WAY
SPURR COURT
Herman Wk.
SADDLEBROOK CT.
MARTIN CHEESEMAN CT.
8
HOUNDSWAY
THE GALLOPS
WALKER DR.
EATON COURT
INVICTA COURT
VINCENT WAY
BRADLEY DRIVE
HINTON AVENUE
LANE
REDCOAT WAY
WAY
WILLOUGHBY WAY
LYDHAM COURT
OSPREY CLO.
DR.
PHEASANT DRI.
SHERRINGHAM DR.
CARRFIELD
FOXTON
ACOMB WOOD CL.
ASHBOURNE WAY
CHANTRY CL.
DEEPDALE
AVENUE
ASHMEADE CLO.
WOOD
TORRIDON PL.
WALK
ALNESS
DEVERON
RYECROFT
ARUNDEL GR.
ULLSWATER
SUMMERFIELD ROAD
ASKHAM
Acomb Wood
LOWICK
TROUTBECK
WORDSWORTH CRESCENT
HALLADALE CLO.
DRIVE
ACOMB
9
SKIDDAW
BANNISDALE
STONETHWAITE
Playing Fields
KINBRACE DRI.
Acomb Park
TARBERT CRES.
WAY
NEVIS
COESIDE
ALNESS
GIRVAN
CL.
DEE CL.
EDEN
GRASSHOLME
MITERDALE
LINDALE
IRVINE WAY
ETIVE PL.
CARRON CRES.
BURNSALL CT.
HELMSDALE
ORRIN CL.
WAINSBECK
CAIRBOROUGH
DRIVE
DALMALLY
CLOSE
QUAKER GRN.
CRUMMOCK
NAIRN CL.
MOOR
CLOSE
SPEY BANK
MOOR
LANE
ANNAN CL.
A
B
LANE

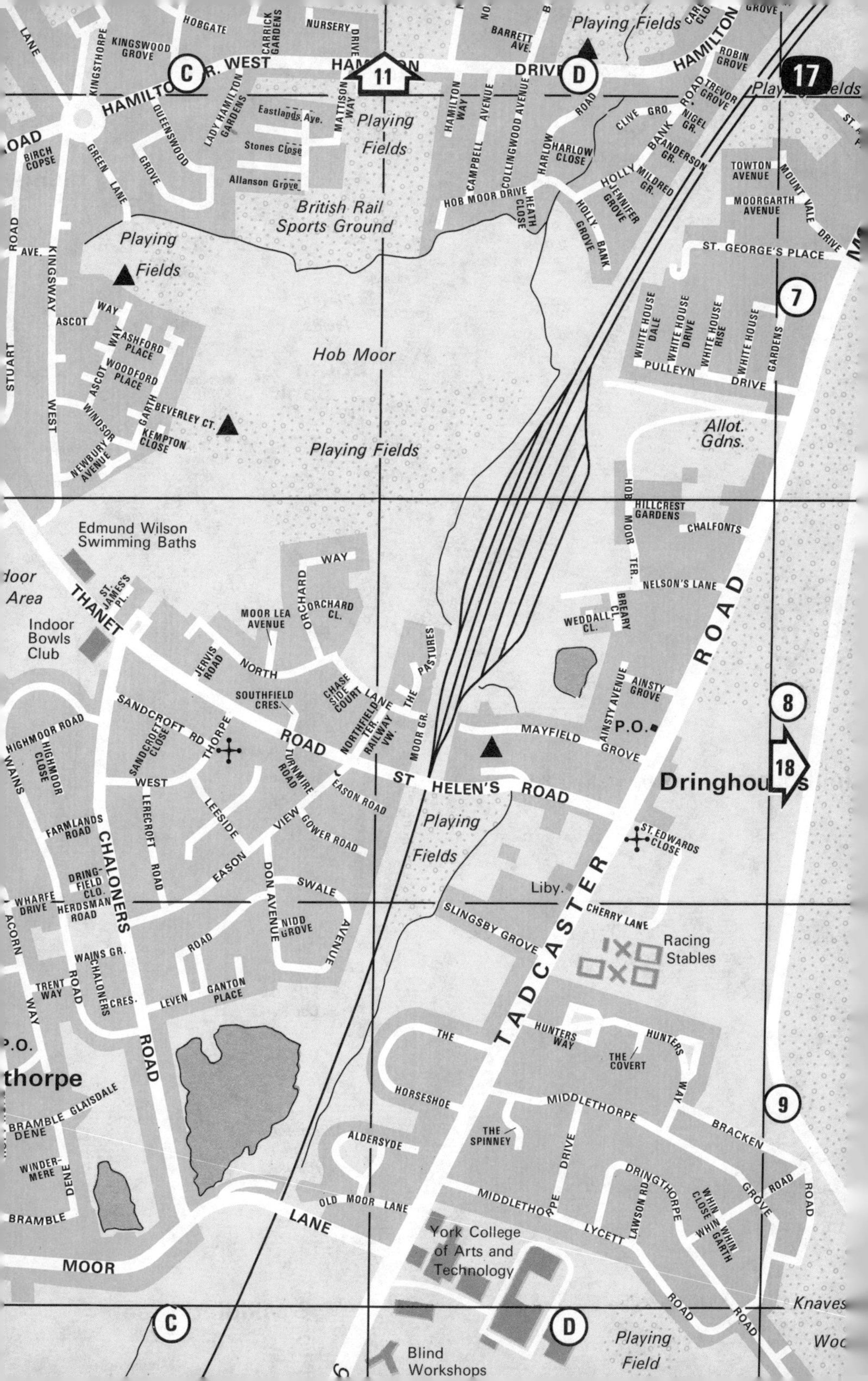

HOBGATE
KINGSWOOD GROVE
CARRICK GARDENS
NURSERY DRIVE
BARRETT AVE.
Playing Fields
HAMILTON DRIVE WEST
HAMILTON DRIVE
11
C
D
17
Playing Fields
ROBIN GROVE
TREVOR GROVE
KINGSTHORPE
QUEENSWOOD GROVE
LADY HAMILTON GARDENS
Eastlands Ave.
Stones Close
Allanson Grove
MATTISON WAY
Playing Fields
British Rail Sports Ground
HAMILTON WAY
CAMPBELL AVENUE
COLLINGWOOD AVENUE
HARLOW ROAD
HARLOW CLOSE
HOB MOOR DRIVE
HEATH CLOSE
CLIVE GRO.
BANK ROAD
NIGEL GR.
ANDERSON GR.
HOLLY BANK GROVE
JENNIFER GROVE
MILDRED GR.
TOWTON AVENUE
MOORGARTH AVENUE
MOUNT VALE DRIVE
ST. GEORGE'S PLACE
BIRCH COPSE
GREEN LANE
STUART ROAD
KINGSWAY WEST
Playing Fields
ASCOT WAY
ASHFORD PLACE
WOODFORD PLACE
WINDSOR GARTH
BEVERLEY CT.
KEMPTON CLOSE
NEWBURY AVENUE
Hob Moor
Playing Fields
WHITE HOUSE DALE
WHITE HOUSE DRIVE
WHITE HOUSE RISE
WHITE HOUSE GARDENS
PULLEYN DRIVE
7
Allot. Gdns.
Edmund Wilson Swimming Baths
Indoor Area
Indoor Bowls Club
THANET ROAD
ST. JAMES'S PL.
ORCHARD WAY
ORCHARD CL.
MOOR LEA AVENUE
JERVIS ROAD
NORTH LANE
SOUTHFIELD CRES.
CHASE SIDE COURT
NORTHFIELD TER.
RAILWAY VW.
THE PASTURES
MOOR GR.
HOB MOOR TER.
HILLCREST GARDENS
CHALFONTS
NELSON'S LANE
WEDDALL CL.
BREARY CL.
AINSTY AVENUE
AINSTY GROVE
MAYFIELD GROVE
P.O.
8
18
Dringhouses
HIGHMOOR ROAD
HIGHMOOR CLOSE
SANDCROFT RD
SANDCROFT CLOSE
THORPE WEST
TURNMIRE ROAD
ST HELEN'S ROAD
EASON ROAD
EASON VIEW
GOWER ROAD
Playing Fields
WAINS ROAD
FARMLANDS ROAD
LERECROFT ROAD
LEESIDE
ST. EDWARDS CLOSE
Liby.
DRINGFIELD CLO.
WHARFE DRIVE
HERDSMAN ROAD
CHALONERS ROAD
DON AVENUE
SWALE AVENUE
NIDD GROVE
SLINGSBY GROVE
CHERRY LANE
ACORN WAY
WAINS GR.
TRENT WAY
CHALONERS CRES.
LEVEN ROAD
GANTON PLACE
Racing Stables
TADCASTER ROAD
P.O.
Woodthorpe
THE HORSESHOE
HUNTERS WAY
THE COVERT
BRAMBLE DENE
GLAISDALE
WINDERMERE
MIDDLETHORPE DRIVE
BRACKEN ROAD
9
THE SPINNEY
ALDERSYDE
DRINGTHORPE ROAD
WHIN CLOSE
WHIN GARTH
GROVE ROAD
OLD MOOR LANE
MOOR LANE
BRAMBLE
LAWSON RD
LYCETT ROAD
York College of Arts and Technology
Knavesmire
Wood
Playing Field
Blind Workshops

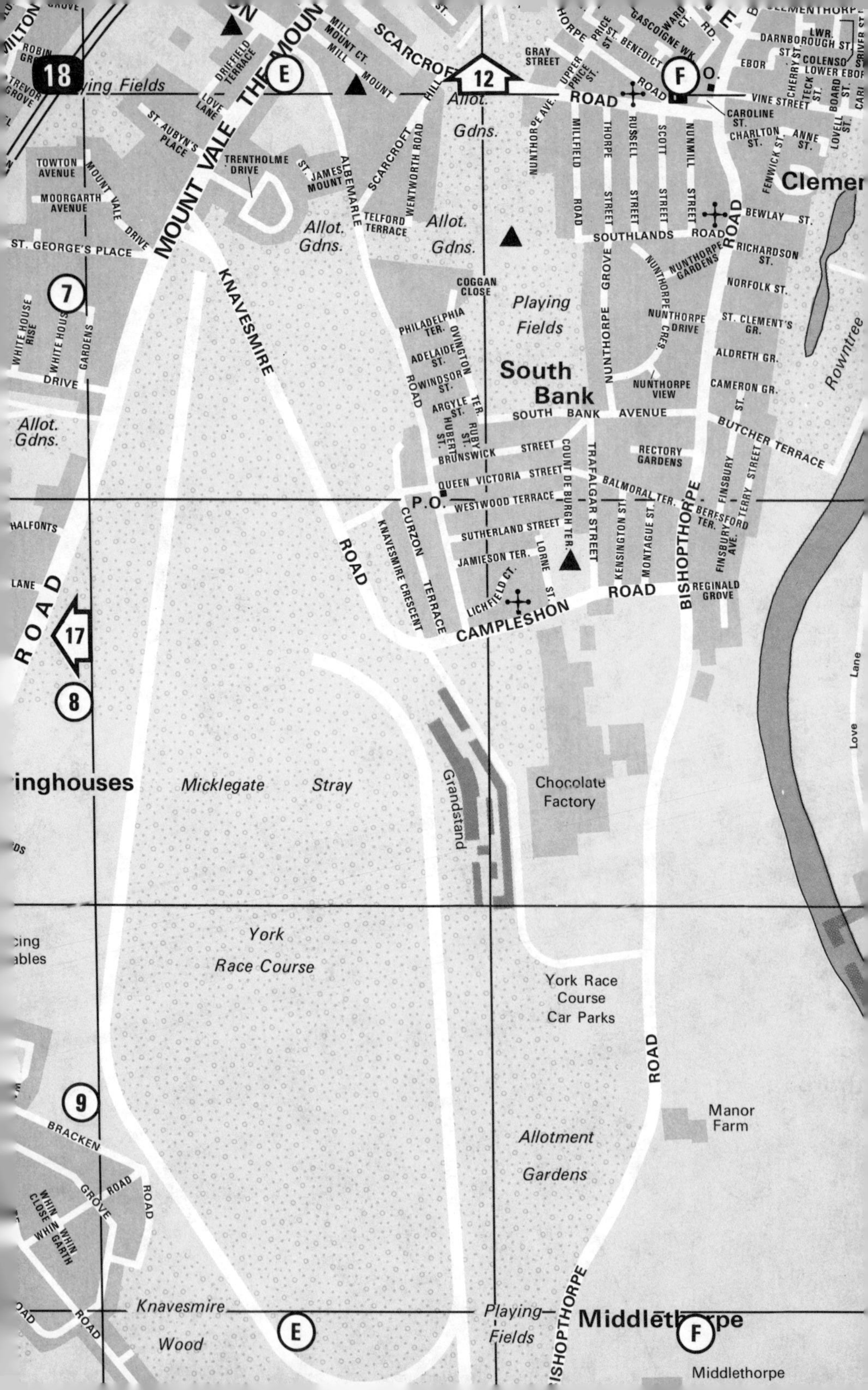

Playing Fields
DRIFFIELD TERRACE
LOVE LANE
THE MOUNT
MOUNT VALE
ST. AUBYN'S PLACE
TRENTHOLME DRIVE
ST. JAMES MOUNT
MILL MOUNT CT.
MILL MOUNT
SCARCROFT HILL
SCARCROFT ROAD
ALBEMARLE ROAD
WENTWORTH ROAD
TELFORD TERRACE
12
Allot. Gdns.
TOWTON AVENUE
MOORGARTH AVENUE
MOUNT VALE DRIVE
ST. GEORGE'S PLACE
ROBIN GROVE
TREVOR GROVE
WHITE HOUSE RISE
WHITE HOUSE GARDENS
DRIVE
KNAVESMIRE ROAD
GRAY STREET
UPPER PRICE ST.
PRICE ST.
NUNTHORPE AVE.
NUNTHORPE ROAD
MILLFIELD ROAD
THORPE STREET
RUSSELL STREET
SCOTT STREET
NUNMILL STREET
ST. BENEDICT ROAD
GASCOIGNE WK.
WARD CT.
P.O.
VINE STREET
CAROLINE ST.
CHARLTON ST.
ANNE ST.
FENWICK ST.
EBOR
DARNBOROUGH ST.
LWR. DARNBOROUGH ST.
COLENSO
LOWER EBOR
CHERRY ST.
TECK ST.
BOARD ST.
LOVELL ST.
Clemen
BEWLAY ST.
SOUTHLANDS ROAD
RICHARDSON ST.
NUNTHORPE GARDENS
NUNTHORPE CRES.
NUNTHORPE DRIVE
NUNTHORPE GROVE
NUNTHORPE VIEW
NORFOLK ST.
ST. CLEMENT'S GR.
ALDRETH GR.
CAMERON GR.
Rowntree
COGGAN CLOSE
Playing Fields
PHILADELPHIA TER.
ADELAIDE ST.
WINDSOR ST.
OVINGTON TER.
ARGYLE ST.
HUBERT ST.
RUBY ST.
South Bank
SOUTH BANK AVENUE
BUTCHER TERRACE
BRUNSWICK STREET
COUNT DE BURGH TER.
TRAFALGAR STREET
RECTORY GARDENS
QUEEN VICTORIA STREET
BALMORAL TER.
FINSBURY STREET
TERRY STREET
WESTWOOD TERRACE
BERESFORD TER.
FINSBURY AVE.
SUTHERLAND STREET
KENSINGTON ST.
MONTAGUE ST.
BISHOPTHORPE ROAD
JAMIESON TER.
LORNE ST.
LICHFIELD CT.
CAMPLESHON ROAD
REGINALD GROVE
CURZON TERRACE
KNAVESMIRE CRESCENT
HALFONTS
LANE
ROAD
17
ringhouses
Micklegate Stray
Grandstand
Chocolate Factory
Love Lane
York Race Course
cing ables
York Race Course Car Parks
ROAD
Manor Farm
Allotment Gardens
BRACKEN ROAD
GROVE ROAD
WHIN CLOSE
WHIN GARTH
Knavesmire Wood
Playing Fields
Middlethorpe
BISHOPTHORPE
Middlethorpe
7
8
9
E
F

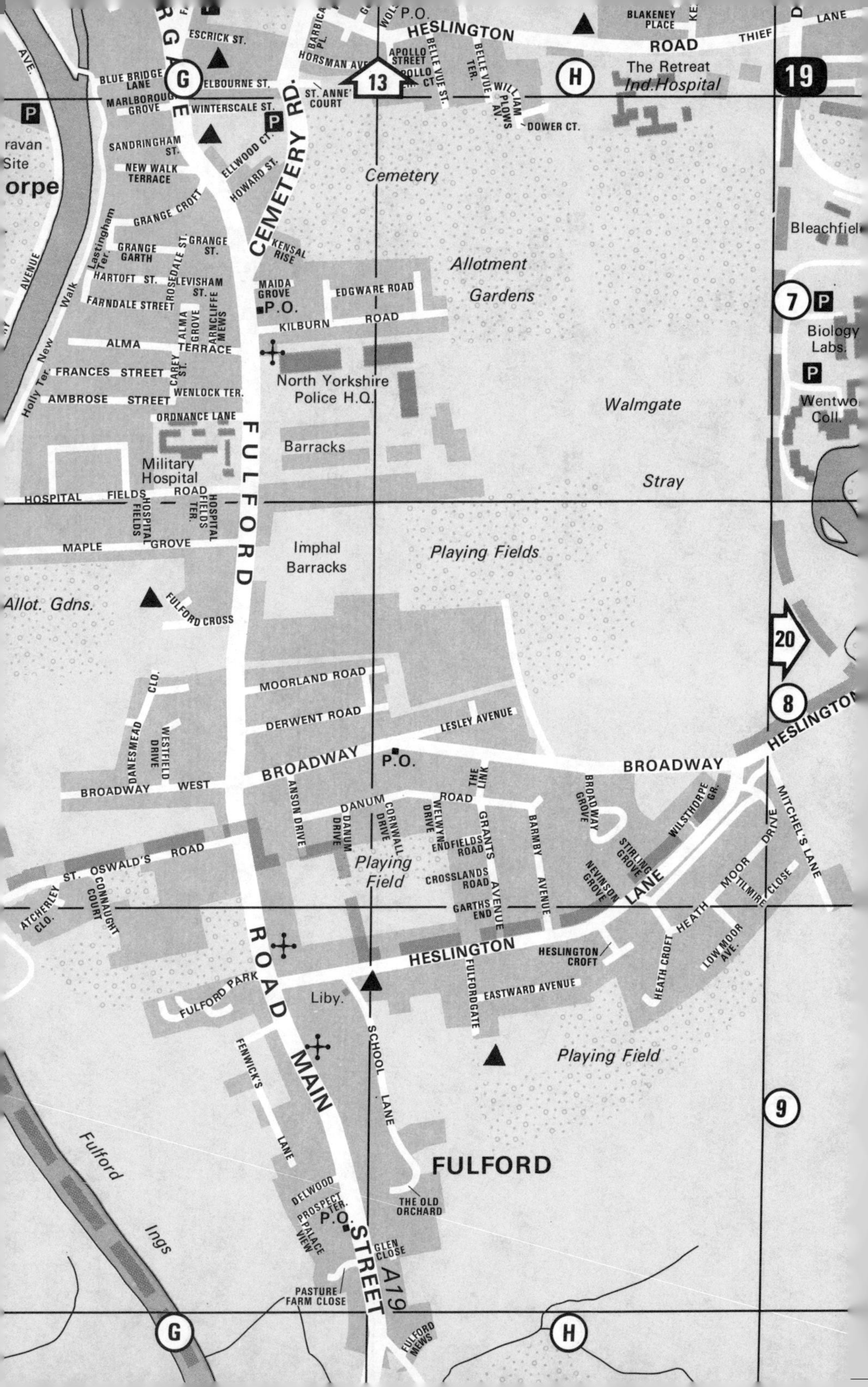
ESCRICK ST.
P.O.
HESLINGTON
BLAKENEY PLACE
ROAD
THIEF
LANE
BARBICAN PL.
HORSMAN AVE.
APOLLO STREET
APOLLO CT.
BELLE VUE ST.
BELLE VUE TER.
WILLIAM PLOWS AV.
DOWER CT.
The Retreat
Ind. Hospital
13
19
G
H
AVE.
BLUE BRIDGE LANE
ELBOURNE ST.
MARLBOROUGH GROVE
WINTERSCALE ST.
ST. ANNE' COURT
P
ravan Site
orpe
SANDRINGHAM ST.
NEW WALK TERRACE
ELLWOOD CT.
HOWARD ST.
CEMETERY RD.
Cemetery
GRANGE CROFT
Lastingham Ter.
GRANGE GARTH
ROSEDALE ST.
GRANGE ST.
KENSAL RISE
Allotment
Gardens
Bleachfiel
HARTOFT ST.
LEVISHAM ST.
MAIDA GROVE
EDGWARE ROAD
P.O.
FARNDALE STREET
ARNCLIFFE MEWS
ALMA GROVE
AVENUE
Walk
New
KILBURN ROAD
7
Biology Labs.
ALMA TERRACE
FRANCES STREET
CAREY ST.
North Yorkshire Police H.Q.
AMBROSE STREET
WENLOCK TER.
Holly Ter.
Walmgate
Wentwo Coll.
ORDNANCE LANE
FULFORD
Barracks
Military Hospital
Stray
HOSPITAL FIELDS ROAD
HOSPITAL FIELDS
HOSPITAL FIELDS TER.
MAPLE GROVE
Imphal Barracks
Playing Fields
Allot. Gdns.
FULFORD CROSS
20
MOORLAND ROAD
CLO.
8
DERWENT ROAD
LESLEY AVENUE
HESLINGTON
DANESMEAD
WESTFIELD DRIVE
BROADWAY
P.O.
BROADWAY
THE LINK
BROADWAY WEST
ANSON DRIVE
DANUM ROAD
DANUM DRIVE
CORNWALL DRIVE
WELWYN DRIVE
GRANTS AVENUE
BARMBY AVENUE
BROADWAY GROVE
WILSTHORPE GR.
MITCHEL'S LANE
ENDFIELDS ROAD
ST. OSWALD'S ROAD
Playing Field
STIRLING GROVE
CROSSLANDS ROAD
NEVINSON GROVE
MOOR DRIVE
ATCHERLEY CLO.
CONNAUGHT COURT
GARTHS END
LANE
TILMIRE CLOSE
HEATH
ROAD
HESLINGTON
HESLINGTON CROFT
LOW MOOR AVE.
FULFORD PARK
Liby.
FULFORDGATE
EASTWARD AVENUE
HEATH CROFT
MAIN
SCHOOL LANE
Playing Field
FENWICK'S LANE
Fulford
9
Ings
FULFORD
DELWOOD
PROSPECT TER.
THE OLD ORCHARD
P.O.
PALACE VIEW
STREET
GLEN CLOSE
A19
PASTURE FARM CLOSE
FULFORD MEWS

University of York — Heslington Campus Map

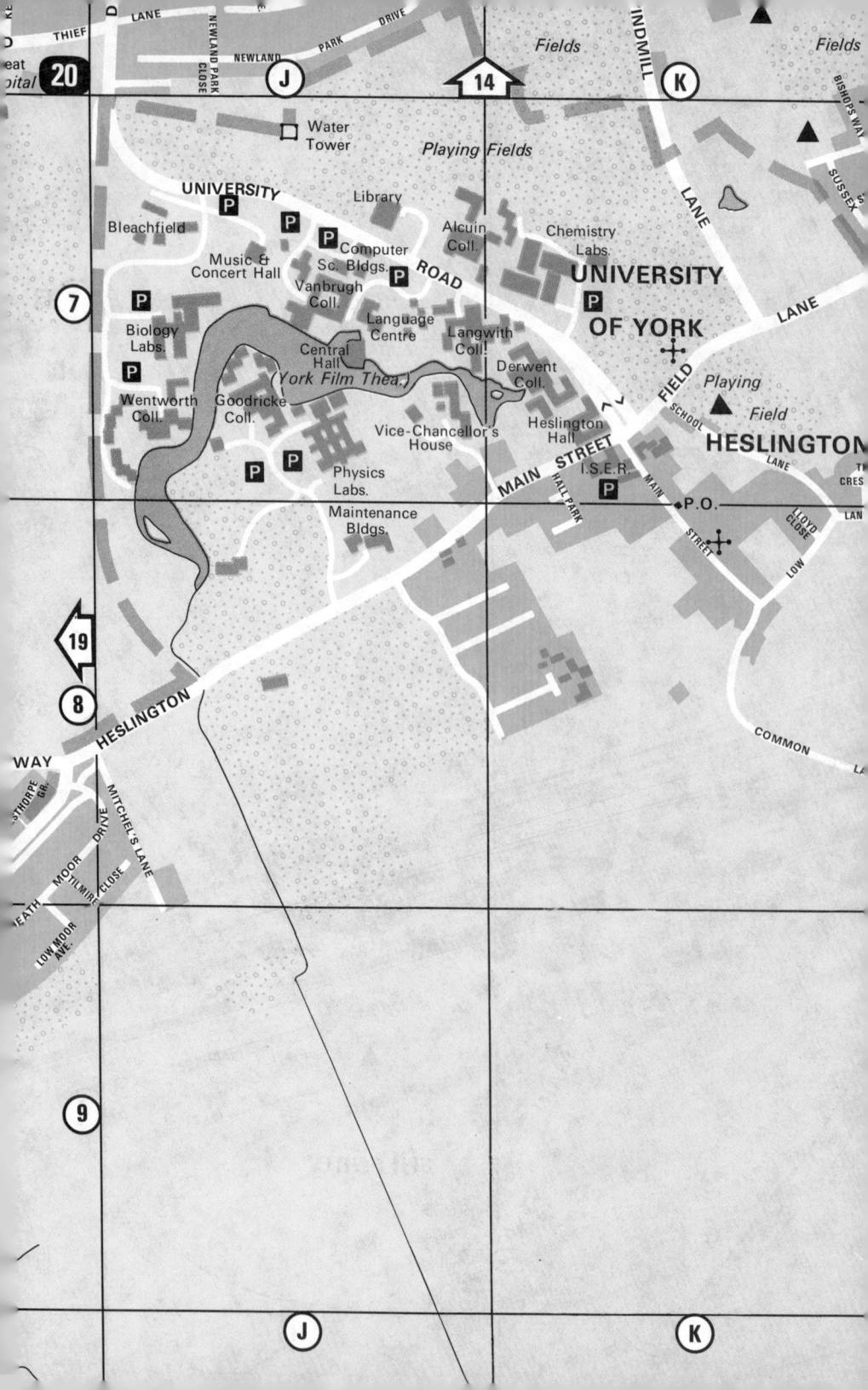

Grid references: J, K (top and bottom); 7, 8, 9 (left side); 14, 19, 20 (direction indicators)

Labelled locations:

- Water Tower
- Playing Fields
- Library
- Bleachfield
- University P (parking)
- Music & Concert Hall
- Computer Sc. Bldgs.
- Vanbrugh Coll.
- Alcuin Coll.
- Chemistry Labs.
- UNIVERSITY OF YORK
- Biology Labs.
- Language Centre
- Langwith Coll.
- Central Hall (York Film Thea.)
- Derwent Coll.
- Wentworth Coll.
- Goodricke Coll.
- Vice-Chancellor's House
- Heslington Hall
- HESLINGTON
- Physics Labs.
- I.S.E.R.
- P.O.
- Maintenance Bldgs.
- Playing Field

Roads / Streets:

- THIEF LANE
- NEWLAND PARK DRIVE
- NEWLAND PARK CLOSE
- WINDMILL LANE
- BISHOPS WAY
- SUSSEX
- UNIVERSITY ROAD
- FIELD LANE
- SCHOOL LANE
- MAIN STREET
- HALL PARK
- LLOYD CLOSE
- LOW LANE
- COMMON LANE
- HESLINGTON
- WAY
- 'STHORPE GR.
- MOOR
- MITCHEL'S LANE
- TILMIRT CLOSE
- LOW MOOR AVE.
- CRES

Places of interest in York

York — A Short History

York, for centuries the northern capital of England, owes its origins to the River Ouse which flows through the old town centre and to the Romans who built the fortress town and named it Eboracum. After their withdrawal in the fifth century it was the Anglo Saxon invaders who took control of the city and built the first cathedral, but these too were ousted when the Vikings captured York and named it Jorvik.

After William the Conqueror defeated Harold at the Battle of Hastings, England was ruled by the Normans and under them York flourished, particularly as a port and a centre for the wool trade. At this time the present city walls and gates were built.

York suffered a decline in the sixteenth century with the dwindling of the wool trade and Henry VIII's dissolution of the monasteries, but it enjoyed a renaissance in the eighteenth century when handsome Georgian houses and buildings began to replace the decayed medieval ones. In the nineteenth and twentieth centuries the city again grew to be as important as ever it had been, becoming a great railway centre and ecclesiastical headquarters.

Assembly Rooms, Blake Street F5 4
Designed by Lord Burlington and paid for by public subscription, these elegant eighteenth-century rooms were the centre of fashionable Georgian society functions, especially in the central hall distinguished by its 48 supporting Corinthian columns.

The Bar Convent Museum, Blossom Street E6 4
A pilgrimage through 300 years of Christian history in York and in the life of England's oldest, active post-reformation convent which has a magnificent domed chapel.

Castle Museum, Tower Street G6 5
A remarkable record of everyday life through the centuries, including the Kirkgate — an authentic reconstruction of a Victorian street complete with shops and houses.

City Art Gallery, Exhibition Square F5 4
Especially noted for its Italian collection the Gallery has works by the York-born artist William Etty and is known for its Lycett Green collection of Old Masters.

Clifford's Tower, Tower Street G6 5
The original wooden castle, built by William the Conqueror, was destroyed by fire in 1190 and the existing stone castle Keep was built in the thirteenth century.

Fairfax House, Castlegate G6 5
Described as a classic architectural masterpiece of its age, this is the finest Georgian town house in York and is furnished with elegant period pieces from the Noel Terry collection of furniture and clocks.

Guildhall, Coney Street F5 4
Badly damaged during an air raid in 1942 the Guildhall is a restoration of the original fifteenth-century Commonhall, although the Inner Chamber escaped serious damage in 1942 and is worth visiting.

Jorvik Viking Centre, Coppergate F5 4
This exact reconstruction of a Viking street is built on the site of the original archaeological excavation and visitors are taken through it in 'time cars' from which they experience the authentic sights, sounds and smells of Jorvik — Viking York.

Kings Manor, Exhibition Square F5 4
Originally the home of the Abbot of St. Mary's Abbey, it became the official residence of the King's Council of the North after the dissolution of the monasteries and is now part of the University of York.

The Mansion House, St. Helen's Square F5 4
Built in the eighteenth century this is the official residence of the Lord Mayor of York, during his term of office and also contains the civic plate.

Merchant Adventurers' Hall, Fossgate G5 5
This magnificent, timbered, medieval Guild Hall, which was built in the fourteenth century, is one of the best surviving examples and is noted for its fine timbered roof in the Great Hall.

Merchant Taylors' Hall, Aldwark G5 5
Built in the fourteenth century this timber-roofed hall has been used by the Company of Merchant Taylors since the fifteenth century and although it was disused for many years has been completely restored by the Guild.

National Railway Museum, Leeman Road E5 4
Part of London's Science Museum, the Railway Museum has one of the finest collections of British railway engineering heritage in Britain, if not the world and in the Great Hall an historic collection of locomotives and rolling stock (including Queen Victoria's Saloon) are arranged around two original turntables.

St. Anthony's Hall, Peasholme Green G5 5
This medieval Guildhall, built in the fifteenth century, is now the Borthwick Institute of Historical Research, part of the University of York.

St. Leonard's Hospital, Museum Street F5 4
Only ruins remain of this eleventh-century hospital which was rebuilt after a fire in the twelfth century and suppressed by Henry VIII.

St. Mary's Abbey, Museum Gardens F5 4
Originally founded in 1080 as a Benedictine Abbey, the existing ruins date from the medieval period and form part of the setting for the medieval 'Mystery Plays' which are re-enacted in the Museum Gardens.

St. William's College, College Street G5 5
This timbered, fifteenth-century building was originally a college for Minster Chantry priests until its dissolution by Henry VIII a century later. During the Civil War Charles I had his printing press and Royal Mint housed here.

Treasurer's House, Minster Yard G5 5
Set on the site of old Roman barracks, the original house was the home of the Treasurers of York Minster, but only part of this remains and the present house, which dates from the seventeenth and eighteenth centuries, has a collection of pictures and furniture from many periods.

Twelfth Century House, Stonegate F5 4
These fragmentary remains of a Norman house have been restored and are the oldest existing in York.

Wax Museum, Lower Friargate E6 5
A collection of more than 50 wax models of famous people including such tableaux as the 'Dukes of York' and the 'Royal Family'.

Yorkshire Museum, Museum Gardens F5 4
Situated in the botanic gardens, where there is also an astronomical observatory, the museum houses impressive collections of archaeology, natural history, geology and pottery, including excellent displays of Roman and medieval treasures.

Yorkshire Museum of Farming, Murton (2 miles east of York)
This museum traces the history of farming developments and has demonstrations of country crafts.

York Story Heritage Centre, Castlegate G6 5
The history and architecture of the city explored through the use of models, reconstructions and audio-visual presentations.

York Minster F5 5
The triple towers of the great Minster dominate York. The fifth church to stand upon the site, it is built in cruciform style and its chief characteristics, inside as outside, are great beauty and impressive size and space. The magnificent stained glass in the Minster — much of it medieval — is of tremendous interest. In the south transept the great Rose window displays a design entwining the red and white roses of Lancaster and York respectively, and commemorates the wedding in 1486 of Henry VII to Elizabeth of York, which at last united the two warring 'Roses'. The Choir, the north transept, and the octagonal Chapter House are very fine, the roof vaulting being among the best examples to be seen anywhere. Beyond the Close to the north of the Minster are the Deanery and the Library (Early English), the latter the repository of many literary treasures. The Minster itself is rich in historic possessions and is the seat of the second See of England, its Archbishop being next in rank and precedence to the Primate of All England, the Archbishop of Canterbury.

A fire in 1984 badly damaged the roof of the south transept but brave firefighting prevented it spreading to the rest of the Cathedral.

City Walls and Bars
Extending for three miles around the city, the walls and gateways built in the thirteenth century by the Normans have withstood the efforts of City Councils to demolish them for building purposes and now provide a fascinating walk affording fine views over the city.

YORK MINSTER

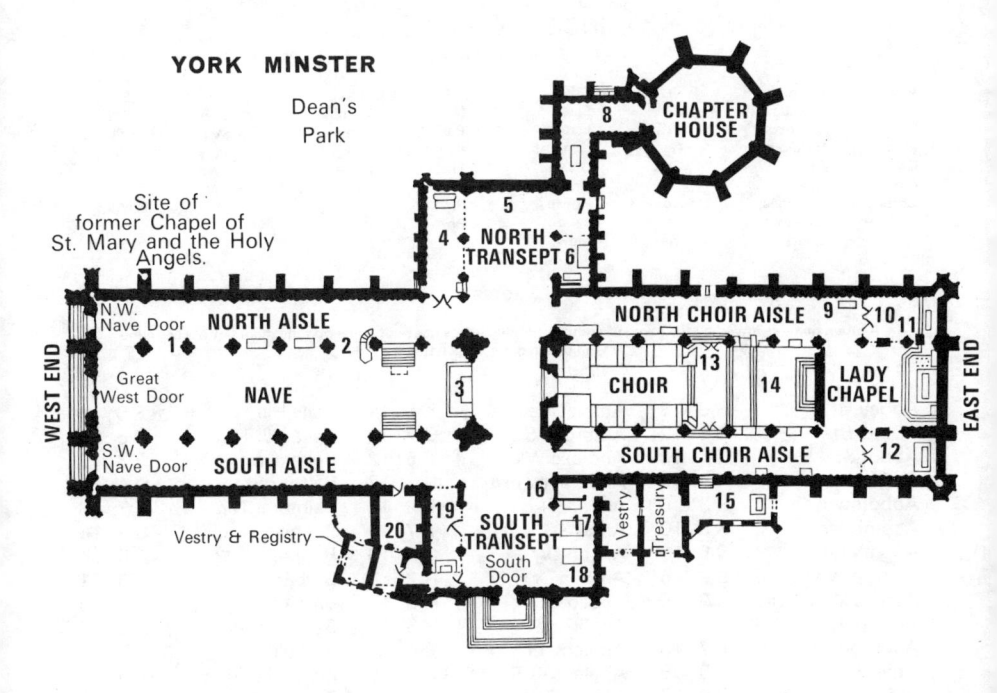

(Floor plan of York Minster showing: Dean's Park; Site of former Chapel of St. Mary and the Holy Angels; Chapter House; North Transept; North Aisle; Nave; South Aisle; North Choir Aisle; Choir; Lady Chapel; South Choir Aisle; South Transept; Vestry & Registry; South Door; West End with Great West Door, N.W. Nave Door, S.W. Nave Door; East End; Vestry/Treasury)

1. Altar of The Lord's Prayer
2. Nave Pulpit
3. Nave Altar
4. St. John's Chapel
5. Five Sisters Window
6. St. Nicholas' Chapel
7. Astronomical Clock
8. Vestibule
9. Effigy of Prince William of Hatfield
10. St. Stephen's Chapel
11. Tomb of Archbishop Scrope
12. All Saints' Chapel
13. Entrance to Crypt
14. High Altar
15. Zouche Chapel
16. Archbishop Thomson Monument
17. Tomb of Archbishop Walter de Grey
18. Dean Duncombe Monument
19. St. George's Chapel
20. Bookshop

INDEX TO STREETS
General Abbreviations

App.	Approach	Dr.	Drive	Mt.	Mount	St.	Street
Av.	Avenue	E.	East	N.	North	Ter.	Terrace
Bdy.	Broadway	Est.	Estate	Par.	Parade	Vills.	Villas
Bldgs.	Buildings	Gdns.	Gardens	Pk.	Park	Vw.	View
Cft.	Croft	Grn.	Green	Pl.	Place	W.	West
Clo.	Close	Gro.	Grove	Prom.	Promenade	Wk.	Walk
Cotts.	Cottages	Ho.	House	Ri.	Rise	Yd.	Yard
Cres.	Crescent	La.	Lane	Rd.	Road		
Ct.	Court	Ms.	Mews	S.	South		

NOTES

A street name followed by the name of another street in italics does not appear on the map, but will be found adjoining or near the latter.

Abbey Ct.	H 3 8	Ambleside Av.	K 5 14	Baile Hill	F 6 4
Abbey St.	E 4 12	Ambrose St.	G 7 19	Baile Hill Ter.	F 6 4
Abbot St.	G 4 13	Ancress Wk.	F 6 12	Baker St.	F 3 7
Abbotsford Rd.	H 6 13	Anderson Gro.	D 7 17	Balfour St.	D 4 11
Abbotsway	H 3 8	Annan Clo.	B 9 16	Balmoral Ter.	F 7 18
Acomb Ms.	B 6 10	Anne St.	F 7 18	Bannisdale	B 9 16
Acomb Rd.	C 5 11	Anson Dr.	G 8 19	Bar La.	E 6 4
Acomb Wood Clo.	B 9 16	Anthea Dr.	H 2 8	Barbara Gro.	D 6 11
Acomb Wood Dr.	A 9 16	Apollo Ct.	H 6 13	Barbican Pl.	G 6 13
Acorn Way	C 9 17	Apollo St.	H 6 13	Barbican Rd.	G 6 5
Adelaide St.	E 7 18	Appleby Pl.	J 5 14	Barfield Rd.	H 2 8
Agar St.	G 5 5	Applecroft Rd.	K 3 9	Barker La.	F 6 4
Ainsty Av.	D 8 17	Argyle St.	E 7 18	Barkston Av.	A 6 10
Ainsty Gro.	D 8 17	Arncliffe Mews	G 7 19	Barkston Clo.	A 6 10
Albany St.	D 5 11	Arnside Pl.	H 6 13	Barkston Gro.	A 6 10
Albemarle Rd.	E 7 18	Arran Pl.	G 3 8	Barkston Rd.	A 6 10
Albert St.	G 6 5	Arthur St.	H 6 13	Barleycorn Yd.	G 6 5
Albion Av.	A 4 10	Arundel Gro.	B 9 16	Barlow St.	C 5 11
Albion St.	F 6 4	Ascot Way	C 7 17	Barmby Av.	H 8 19
Alcelina Ct.	F 6 12	Ash Clo.	K 3 9	Barrett Av.	D 6 11
Alcuin Av.	J 6 14	Ash St.	D 5 11	Barstow Av.	J 6 14
Aldersyde	C 9 17	Ashbourne Way	B 9 16	Baysdale Av.	L 6 15
Aldreth Gro.	F 7 18	Ashford Pl.	C 7 17	Beaconsfield St.	B 6 10
Aldwark	G 5 5	Ashley Park Cres.	K 4 14	Beagle Ridge Dr.	B 8 16
Alexander Av.	H 1 8	Ashley Park Rd.	K 3 9	Beans Way	K 3 9
Alexandra Ct.	H 5 13	Ashmeade Clo.	A 9 16	Beck La.	J 4 14
Algarth Rd.	K 3 9	Ashton Av.	F 2 7	Beckfield La.	A 5 10
Algarth Ri.	K 3 9	Ashville St.	G 3 8	Beckfield Pl.	A 5 10
All Saints La.	F 5 4	Askham Gro.	A 7 16	Beckwith Clo.	K 3 9
Allanson Gro.	C 7 17	Askham La.	A 9 16	Bedale Av.	L 5 15
Allen Clo.	J 6 14	Asquith Av.	J 5 14	Bede Av.	F 3 7
Allendale	B 8 16	Atcherley Clo.	G 9 19	Bedern	G 5 5
Allington Dr.	K 4 14	Avenue Rd.	E 4 12	Beech Av.	D 6 11
Alma Gro.	G 7 19	Avenue Ter.	E 4 12	Beech Glade	H 1 8
Alma Ter.	G 7 19	Avenue, The	E 4 12	Beech Gro.	B 5 10
Almery Ter.	E 5 4			Beechwood Glade	A 8 16
Almsford Dr.	B 4 10	Bachelor Hill	B 6 10	Belgrave St.	F 3 7
Almsford Rd.	B 4 10	Back La.	A 5 10	Bell Farm Av.	G 2 8
Alne Ter.	G 6 13	Back Swinegate	F 5 5	Belle Vue St.	H 6 13
Alness Clo.	A 9 16	Back West Vw.	F 3 7	Belle Vue Ter.	H 6 13
Alvis Gro.	L 5 15	Backhouse St.	F 4 12	Bellhouse Way	B 8 16
Alwyne Dr.	C 2 6	Bad Bargain La.	J 4 14	Belmont Clo.	D 2 6
Alwyne Gro.	C 2 6	Badger Paddock	H 1 8	Beresford Ter.	F 8 18
Amber St.	G 4 13	Badger Wood Wk.	L 9 15	Berkeley Ter.	C 5 11
Amberly St.	C 5 11	Baildon Clo.	C 6 11	Beverley Ct.	C 7 17

24

Name	Grid		Name	Grid		Name	Grid	
Beverley Gdns.	H 4	13	Brompton Rd.	E 3	7	Cedarwood Clo.	A 8	16
Bewlay St.	F 7	18	Brook St.	F 4	12	Celtic Clo.	B 4	10
Bilsdale Clo.	D 1	6	Brooklands	L 5	15	Cemetery Rd.	G 7	19
Birch Copse	C 7	17	Broughton Way	K 5	14	Chalfonts	D 8	17
Birkdale Gro.	A 5	10	Browney Cft.	G 6	13	Chaloners Cres.	C 9	17
Birstwith Dr.	C 5	11	Brownlow St.	G 4	13	Chaloners Rd.	C 8	17
Bishopgate St.	F 6	4	Brunswick St.	E 7	18	Chantry Clo.	B 9	16
Bishophill Junior	F 6	4	Buckingham St.	F 6	4	Chapel Fields Rd.	A 6	10
Bishophill Senior	F 6	4	Bull La., Heworth	H 4	13	Chapel Row	G 6	5
Bishops Way	K 6	14	Bull La.	H 6	13	Chapter House St.	F 5	5
Bishopthorpe Rd.	F 9	18	Bur Dike Av.	E 3	7	Charles Moor	J 3	9
Bismarck St.	D 4	11	Burgess Wk.	B 8	16	Charlotte St.	H 6	13
Blackthorne Dr.	H 1	8	Burlington Av.	J 6	14	Charlton St.	F 7	18
Blake St.	F 5	4	Burnholme Av.	J 4	14	Chaseside Ct.	C 8	17
Blakeney Pl.	H 6	13	Burnholme Dr.	J 4	14	Chatsworth Ter.	C 5	11
Bland La.	A 6	10	Burnholme Gro.	J 4	14	Chaucer St.	H 6	13
Blossom St.	E 6	4	Burniston Gro.	J 6	14	Chelwood Wk.	D 5	11
Blue Bridge La.	G 6	13	Burns Ct.	A 9	16	Cherry Garth	K 4	14
Bootham	F 4	4	Burnsall Dr.	C 6	11	Cherry Hill La.	F 6	12
Bootham Bar	F 5	4	Burrill Av.	F 3	7	Cherry La.	D 9	17
Bootham Cres.	F 4	12	Burton Av.	F 3	7	Cherry St.	F 6	12
Bootham Row	F 4	4	Burton Stone La.	F 3	7	Chestnut Av.	J 4	14
Bootham Sq.	F 4	12	Butcher Ter.	F 7	18	Chestnut Gro.	B 6	10
Bootham Ter.	E 4	4	Buttermere Dr.	C 2	6	Chudleigh Rd.	D 4	11
Boroughbridge Rd.	B 4	10	Byland Av.	H 2	8	Church La.	F 5	4
Borrowdale Dr.	D 2	6	Byron Dr.	D 2	6	Church Rd.	L 5	15
Bouthwaite Dr.	C 5	11				Church St.	F 5	5
Bowes Av.	H 5	13	Caedmon Clo.	J 3	9	Cinder La.	E 5	4
Bowland Way	E 2	7	Cairnborough	A 9	16	Cinder La.,	H 4	13
Bowling Green La.	G 4	13	Caldbeck Clo.	E 2	7	Heworth		
Bowness Dr.	C 1	6	Cambridge St.	E 6	12	Claremont Ter.	F 4	12
Bracken Hill	L 6	15	Cameron Gro.	F 7	18	Clarence St.	F 4	12
Bracken Rd.	D 9	17	Campbell Av.	D 7	17	Clarendon Ct.	F 3	7
Bradley Dr.	B 8	16	Campbell Ct.	K 5	14	Clarendon St.	G 3	8
Braeside Gdns.	C 6	11	Campleshon Rd.	E 8	18	Clarks Ter.	J 4	14
Bramble Dene	C 9	17	Canham Gro.	L 6	15	Clay Pl.	B 6	16
Bramham Av.	A 6	10	Carey St.	G 7	19	Claygate	K 4	14
Bramham Gro.	A 6	10	Carl St.	F 7	18	Clementhorpe	F 6	12
Bramham Rd.	A 6	10	Carleton St.	D 5	11	Cleveland St.	D 6	11
Bramley Garth	K 4	14	Carlisle St.	D 5	11	Clifford St.	F 6	5
Brandsby Gro.	G 1	8	Carlton Av.	K 6	14	Clifton	E 4	12
Bransdale Cres.	L 6	15	Carmelite St.	G 5	5	Clifton Dale	E 4	12
Branton Pl.	A 6	10	Carnot St.	D 4	11	Clifton Grn.	E 4	12
Breary Clo.	D 8	17	Carnoustie Clo.	A 5	10	Clifton Pl.	E 3	7
Brentwood Cres.	L 9	15	Caroline Clo.	D 6	11	Clive Gro.	D 7	17
Bretgate	G 6	5	Caroline St.	F 7	18	Cloisters Wk.	G 5	5
Briar Av.	A 6	10	Carr La.	B 5	10	Close, The	D 2	6
Briar Dr.	H 1	8	Carrfield	B 8	16	Coeside	A 9	16
Bridge La.	F 4	12	Carrick Gdns.	C 6	11	Coffee Yd.	F 5	5
Bridge St.	F 6	4	Carrington Av.	C 5	11	Coggan Clo.	E 7	18
Bridle Way	A 6	10	Carron Cres.	A 9	16	Cole St.	G 4	13
Briggs St.	G 3	8	Carrs La.	F 6	4	Colenso St.	F 6	12
Bright St.	D 5	11	Carter Av.	H 5	13	College St.	G 5	5
Brinkworth Ter.	H 6	13	Castle Mills Bri.	G 6	5	Colliergate	G 5	5
Broad St.	F 7	18	Castle Wk.	G 6	5	Collingham Pl.	A 6	10
Broadway	G 8	19	Castlegate	F 6	5	Collingwood Av.	D 7	17
Broadway Gro.	H 8	19	Cavendish Gro.	L 6	15	Compton St.	E 4	12
Broadway W.	G 8	19	Caxton Av.	C 4	11	Coney St.	F 5	4
Brockfield Park Dr.	H 1	8	Cayley Clo.	D 2	6	Coniston Clo.	C 1	6
Brockfield Rd.	H 1	8	Cecilia Pl.	E 6	12	Coniston Dr.	K 5	14
Bromley St.	D 4	11	Cedar Gro.	K 3	9	Connaught Ct.	G 8	19

25

Constantine Av.	J 5	14	Deramore Dr. W.	L 6	15	Elwick Gro.	K 6 14
Coopers Yd.	G 6	5	Derwent Av.	J 5	14	Emerald St.	G 4 13
Coppergate	F 5	5	Derwent Rd.	G 8	19	Emmerson St.	H 4 13
Corlett Ct.	B 8	16	Deveron Way	A 9	16	Endfields Rd.	H 8 19
Cornborough Av.	J 4	14	Devon Pl.	H 6	13	Enfield Cres.	D 6 11
Cornlands Rd.	A 7	16	Dewsbury Cotts.	F 6	4	Ennerdale Av.	K 5 14
Cornwall Dr.	H 8	19	Dewsbury Ter.	F 6	4	Escrick St.	G 6 13
Cosmo Av.	J 5	14	Diamond St.	G 4	13	Eskdale Av.	L 6 15
Cottage Ms.	J 4	14	Dickson Rd.	A 8	16	Esplanade, The	E 5 4
Count de Burgh Ter.	F 7	18	Dijon Av.	B 6	10	Etive Pl.	A 9 16
			Dilys Gro.	C 5	11	Etty Av.	J 5 14
Courcey Gro.	B 5	10	Dixon La.	G 6	5	Eva Av.	C 1 6
Covert, The	D 9	17	Dixons Yd.	G 6	5	Evelyn Cres.	F 3 7
Coxlea Gro.	K 4	14	Dodgson Ter.	B 5	10	Exhibition Sq.	F 5 4
Cranbrook Av.	B 5	10	Dodsworth Av.	G 3	8		
Cranbrook Rd.	B 4	10	Doherty Wk.	B 8	16	Faber St.	H 5 13
Crawley Way	K 4	14	Don Av.	C 8	17	Fairfax St.	F 6 4
Crescent, The	E 6	4	Doriam Av.	H 1	8	Fairway	E 3 7
Crescent, The, Heslington	K 7	20	Doriam Dr.	H 1	8	Falconer St.	D 6 11
			Dove St.	F 6	12	Falkland St.	F 6 4
Crichton Av.	F 3	7	Dower Ct.	H 7	19	Falsgrave Cres.	F 3 7
Croft Side	B 6	10	Driffield Ter.	E 6	12	Farfield	B 4 10
Croft Way	B 6	10	Dringfield Clo.	C 8	17	Farmlands Rd.	C 8 17
Crombie Av.	E 3	7	Dringthorpe Rd.	D 9	17	Farndale Av.	L 6 15
Cromer St.	E 3	7	Dudley St.	G 4	13	Farndale St.	G 7 19
Cromwell Rd.	F 6	4	Duncombe Pl.	F 5	4	Farrar St.	H 6 13
Crosslands Rd.	H 8	19	Dundas St.	G 5	5	Fawcett St.	G 6 13
Crossway, The	H 3	8				Fawkes Dr.	B 5 10
Crossways	L 6	15	Earle St.	G 4	13	Feasegate	F 5 5
Crummock	B 9	16	Earlsborough Ter.	E 5	4	Fellbrook Av.	A 6 10
Cumberland St.	F 6	5	Eason Rd.	C 8	17	Fenwick St.	F 7 18
Curzon Ter.	E 8	18	Eason Vw.	C 8	17	Fenwicks La.	G 9 19
Custance Wk.	F 6	4	East Cotts.	D 2	6	Fern St.	G 4 13
Cycle St.	J 6	14	East Mount Rd.	E 6	4	Fern Way	L 6 15
Cygnet St.	F 6	12	East Par.	H 4	13	Fetter La.	F 6 4
			East Way	H 1	8	Feversham Cres.	F 3 7
Dales La.	J 4	14	Eastbourne Gro.	H 4	13	Fewster Way	G 6 13
Dalguise Gro.	G 4	13	Eastern Ter.	H 4	13	Field La., Heslington	K 7 20
Dalmally Clo.	A 9	16	Eastfield Cres.	K 7	20		
Dalton Ter.	E 6	12	Eastfield Ct.	K 7	20	Field La.	L 9 15
Dane Av.	B 5	10	Eastholme Dr.	C 1	6	Field Vw.	F 3 7
Danebury Cres.	B 5	10	Eastlands Av.	C 7	17	Fifth Av.	H 4 13
Danebury Dr.	B 6	10	Eastward Av.	H 9	19	Filey Ter.	F 3 7
Danesfort Av.	B 7	16	Eaton Ct.	B 8	16	Finkle St.	F 5 5
Danesmead Clo.	G 8	19	Ebor St.	F 6	12	Finsbury Av.	F 8 18
Danum Dr.	G 8	19	Eden Clo.	B 9	16	Finsbury St.	F 7 18
Danum Rd.	G 8	19	Edgware Rd.	G 7	19	Fir Heath Clo.	B 8 16
Darnborough St.	F 6	12	Eighth Av.	J 5	14	First Av.	H 4 13
Davygate	F 5	4	Elands Yd.	G 6	5	Firtree Clo.	C 6 11
Davygate Centre	F 5	4	Eldon St.	G 4	13	Firwood Whin	H 1 8
Daysfoot Ct.	H 6	13	Eldon Ter.	G 4	13	Fishergate	G 6 13
De Grey St.	F 4	12	Ellwood Ct.	G 7	19	Fishergate Bar	G 6 5
De Grey Ter.	F 4	12	Elm Gro.	H 1	8	Flavian Gro.	D 3 6
Deangate	F 5	5	Elma Gro.	C 1	6	Flaxman Av.	J 6 14
Dee Clo.	B 9	16	Elmfield Av.	H 2	8	Fleming Av.	H 5 13
Deepdale	B 9	16	Elmfield Ter.	H 3	8	Florence Gro.	C 1 6
Del Pyke	G 4	13	Elmlands Gro.	J 3	9	Forest Gro.	H 4 13
Delwood	G 9	19	Elmpark Vale	J 3	9	Forest Way	H 4 13
Dennis St.	G 6	5	Elmpark Vw.	J 3	9	Foresters Wk.	A 8 16
Dennison St.	G 4	13	Elmpark Way	J 3	9	Forth St.	D 4 11
Deramore Dr.	L 6	15	Elvington Ter.	H 6	13	Foss Bank	G 5 13

Name	Grid		Name	Grid		Name	Grid	
Foss Bri.	G 5	5	Glen Av.	H 4	13	Hampden St.	F 6	4
Foss Islands Rd.	G 5	5	Glen Clo.	H 9	19	Hanover St. E.	D 5	11
Fossbank	G 5	5	Glen Rd.	H 4	13	Hanover St. W.	D 5	11
Fossgate	G 5	5	Glencoe St.	F 3	7	Harcourt St.	H 4	13
Fossway	G 3	8	Glenridding	B 9	16	Harington Av.	H 6	13
Foston Gro.	H 2	8	Goodramgate	G 5	5	Harlow Clo.	D 7	17
Foundry La.	D 5	11	Gordon St.	G 6	13	Harlow Rd.	D 7	17
Fountayne St.	F 3	7	Gormire Av.	H 1	8	Harold Ct.	C 6	11
Fourth Av.	H 5	13	Gorse Paddock	H 1	8	Harrison St.	J 4	14
Fox Covert	H 1	8	Government House Rd.	D 4	11	Hartoft St.	G 7	19
Foxthorn Paddock	L 6	15				Hatfield Wk.	B 8	16
Foxton	B 8	16	Gower Rd.	C 8	17	Haughton Rd.	F 3	7
Foxwood La.	A 8	16	Grange Croft	G 7	19	Hawthorn Gro.	H 4	13
Frances St.	G 7	19	Grange Garth	G 7	19	Hawthorn Spinney	H 1	8
Frederic St.	E 5	4	Grange La.	A 7	16	Hawthorn St.	H 4	13
Freemans Ct.	E 4	12	Grange St.	G 7	19	Hawthorn Ter.	G 1	8
Friargate	F 6	5	Granger Av.	B 6	10	Haxby Rd., New Earswick	G 2	8
Friars Wk.	H 3	8	Granger Pl.	B 6	10			
Front St.	B 6	10	Grantham Dr.	C 6	11	Haxby Rd.	G 4	13
Fulford Cross	G 8	19	Grants Av.	H 8	19	Hazel Garth	K 3	9
Fulford Mews	H 9	19	Granville Ter.	H 6	13	Hazelwood Av.	L 6	15
Fulford Pk.	G 9	19	Grape La.	F 5	5	Healey Gro.	H 2	8
Fulford Rd.	G 7	19	Grasmere Dr.	K 5	14	Heath Clo.	D 7	17
Fulfordgate	H 9	19	Grasmere Gro.	D 2	6	Heath Croft	H 9	19
Furness Dr.	C 1	6	Grassholme	B 9	16	Heath Moor Dr.	H 9	19
			Gray St.	F 6	12	Heather Bank	L 6	15
Gale La.	B 7	16	Grayshon Dr.	A 4	10	Heather Cft.	H 1	8
Gallops, The	A 8	16	Green Clo.	E 2	7	Heathfield Rd.	J 6	14
Galtres Av.	K 3	9	Green Dykes La.	J 6	14	Hebden Ri.	C 6	11
Galtres Gro.	D 3	6	Green La., Acomb	B 6	10	Helmsdale	B 9	16
Galtres Rd.	K 3	9	Green La., Rawcliffe	D 2	6	Hemlock Av.	H 2	8
Ganton Pl.	C 9	17				Hempland Av.	J 4	14
Garbutt Gro.	B 5	10	Green Meadows	J 3	9	Hempland Dr.	J 3	9
Garden Pl.	G 5	5	Green Sward	J 3	9	Hempland La.	J 3	9
Garden St.	G 4	13	Green, The	B 6	10	Herbert St.	H 6	13
Garfield Ter.	D 5	11	Greenborough Av.	A 5	10	Herberts Way	J 3	9
Garland St.	C 5	11	Greencliffe Dr.	E 4	12	Herdsman Rd.	C 9	17
Garlands, The	E 2	7	Greenfield Park Dr.	J 3	9	Herman Wk.	B 8	16
Garnet Ter.	D 4	11	Gresley Ct.	B 5	10	Hesketh Bank	L 6	15
Garrow Hill Av.	J 6	14	Grosvenor Rd.	F 4	12	Heslington Croft	H 9	19
Garth Ter.	F 3	7	Grosvenor Ter.	F 4	12	Heslington La.	H 9	19
Garth Way	G 1	8	Grove La.	G 4	13	Heslington Rd.	H 6	13
Garths End	H 9	19	Grove Ter.	B 6	10	Hessay Pl.	A 6	10
Gascoigne Wk.	F 6	12	Grove Terrace La.	G 4	13	Hetherton St.	E 5	4
George Ct.	G 4	13	Grove Vw.	E 4	12	Hewley Av.	J 5	14
George Hudson St.	F 5	4	Groves Ct.	G 4	13	Heworth Grn.	G 4	13
George St.	G 6	5	Groves La.	G 4	5	Heworth Hall Dr.	J 4	14
Gerard Av.	J 4	14	Guardian Ct.	E 3	7	Heworth Pl.	H 4	13
Giles Av.	J 4	14				Heworth Rd.	H 4	13
Gillamoor Av.	K 5	14	Hadrian Av.	K 6	14	Heworth Village	J 4	14
Gillygate	F 5	4	Haleys Ter.	G 3	8	High Newbiggin St.	G 4	5
Girvan Clo.	A 9	16	Hall Pk.	K 7	20	High Oaks	K 3	9
Givendale Gro.	L 6	15	Halladale Clo.	A 9	16	High Ousegate	F 5	5
Glade, The	K 3	9	Hallfield Rd.	G 5	13	High Petergate	F 5	4
Gladstone St., Acomb	B 6	10	Hambleton Av.	K 5	14	Highcliffe Ct.	E 4	12
			Hambleton Ter.	F 3	7	Highfield	L 6	15
Gladstone St.	G 4	13	Hamilton Dr.	C 6	11	Highmoor Clo.	C 8	17
Gladstone Ter.	H 2	8	Hamilton Dr. E.	D 6	11	Highmoor Rd.	C 8	17
Glaisby Ct.	J 4	14	Hamilton Dr. W.	C 7	17	Highthorn Rd.	H 1	8
Glaisdale	C 9	17	Hamilton Way	D 7	17	Hilbeck Gro.	K 4	14
Glebe Av.	C 5	11	Hammerton Clo.	A 6	10	Hilda Ter.	H 6	13

Hill St.	D 6	11	Jackson St.	G 4	13	Lastingham Ter.	G 7	19
Hill Vw.	K 3	9	James St.	H 6	13	Lavender Gro.	C 5	11
Hillcrest Gdns.	D 8	17	Jamieson Ter.	E 8	18	Lawnswood Dr.	D 2	6
Hillsborough Ter.	F 3	7	Jennifer Gro.	D 7	17	Lawnway	J 3	9
Hinton Av.	B 8	16	Jervis Rd.	C 8	17	Lawrence St.	H 6	13
Hob Moor Dr.	D 7	17	Jewbury	G 5	5	Lawson Rd.	D 9	17
Hob Moor Ter.	D 8	17	John St.	H 4	13	Layerthorpe	G 5	5
Hobgate	C 6	11	Jorvik Clo.	B 5	10	Layerthorpe Bri.	G 5	5
Holgate Bridge Gdns.	E 6	12	Jubbergate	F 5	5	Lead Mill La.	G 6	5
			Jubilee Ter.	D 4	11	Leake St.	H 6	13
Holgate Lodge Dr.	C 6	11	Judges Ct.	F 5	4	Leeman Rd.	D 5	11
Holgate Rd.	D 6	11	Jute Rd.	B 5	10	Leeside	C 8	17
Holly Bank Gro.	D 7	17				Leicester Way	G 6	5
Holly Bank Rd.	D 7	17	Keats Clo.	D 2	6	Lendal	F 5	4
Holly Ter.	G 7	19	Kempton Clo.	C 7	17	Lendal Bri.	F 5	4
Holmfield La.	J 8	20	Kendrew Clo.	H 1	8	Lerecroft Rd.	C 8	17
Holroyd Av.	J 4	14	Kenrick Pl.	B 5	10	Lesley Av.	H 8	19
Hope St.	G 6	5	Kensal Ri.	G 7	19	Leven Rd.	C 9	17
Horner St.	F 3	7	Kensington St.	F 8	18	Levisham St.	G 7	19
Horseshoe, The	D 9	17	Kent St.	G 6	13	Leyes, The	L 6	15
Horsman Av.	G 6	13	Kentmere Dr.	D 2	6	Leyland Rd.	J 4	14
Hospital Fields	G 7	19	Kestrel Wood Way	H 1	8	Lichfield Ct.	E 8	18
Hospital Fields Rd.	G 7	19	Kexby Av.	H 6	13	Lidgett Gro.	B 4	10
Hospital Fields Ter.	G 7	19	Kilburn Rd.	G 7	19	Lilac Av.	K 6	14
Hospital La.	F 4	12	Kimberlows Woods Hill	L 6	15	Lilling Av.	H 2	8
Hotham Av.	A 6	10				Lime Av.	J 3	9
Hothams Ct.	G 6	5	Kinbrace Dr.	A 9	16	Lincoln St.	D 4	11
Houndsway	A 8	16	King St.	F 6	4	Lindale	B 9	16
Howard Dr.	C 1	6	Kings Acre	K 4	14	Linden Gro.	E 2	7
Howard Link	C 1	6	Kings Ct.	G 5	5	Lindley St.	D 6	11
Howard St.	G 7	19	Kings Sq.	G 5	5	Lindsey Av.	C 5	11
Howe Hill Clo.	C 5	11	Kings Staith	F 6	4	Link Av.	F 2	7
Howe Hill Rd.	C 5	11	Kingsland Ter.	D 5	11	Link Rd.	G 1	8
Howe St.	C 6	11	Kingsthorpe	C 6	11	Link, The	H 8	19
Hubert St.	E 7	18	Kingsway N.	E 3	7	Linton St.	C 5	11
Huby Ct.	G 6	5	Kingsway W.	C 7	17	Lister Way	E 3	7
Hudson Cres.	E 3	7	Kingswood Gro.	C 6	11	Little Av.	F 2	7
Hudson St.	F 3	7	Kir Cres.	B 6	10	Little Hallfield Rd.	H 5	13
Hull Rd.	J 6	14	Kirk Vw.	B 6	10	Little Shambles	F 5	5
Hungate	G 5	5	Kirkdale Rd.	L 5	15	Little Stonegate	F 5	4
Hunt Ct.	G 5	5	Kirkham Av.	G 3	8	Livingstone St.	D 5	11
Hunters Way	D 9	17	Kirkstone Dr.	J 4	14	Lloyd Clo.	K 8	20
Huntington New La.	J 1	9	Kitchener St.	G 3	8	Loch Rin Pl.	A 5	10
Huntington Rd.	G 4	13	Knapton La.	A 5	10	Lockwood St.	G 4	13
Huntington Rd., New Earswick	H 1	8	Knavesmire Cres.	E 8	18	Long Close La.	G 6	5
			Knavesmire Rd.	E 7	18	Longfield Ter.	E 5	4
Huntsmans Wk.	A 8	16	Knoll, The	A 7	16	Lord Mayors Wk.	G 4	5
Hursts Yd.	G 6	5	Kyme St.	F 6	4	Lorne St.	F 8	18
Hyrst Gro.	H 4	13				Love La.	E 7	18
			Laburnum Garth	J 2	9	Love La., Fulford	F 8	18
Ingleborough Av.	K 5	14	Lady Hamilton Gdns.	C 7	17	Lovell St.	F 7	18
Ingleton Wk.	J 5	14				Low La.	K 8	20
Ingram Av.	F 2	7	Lady Peckitts Yd.	G 5	5	Low Mill Clo.	L 6	15
Ings Vw.	C 1	6	Lady Rd.	F 3	7	Low Moor Av.	H 9	19
Ings Way	D 3	6	Lamel St.	J 6	14	Low Ousegate	F 5	4
Inman Ter.	C 5	11	Landing La.	D 4	11	Low Petergate	F 5	5
Intake Av.	F 3	7	Lang Av.	J 5	14	Low Poppleton La.	B 4	10
Invicta Ct.	B 8	16	Langdale Av.	K 4	14	Lower Darnborough St.	F 6	12
Irvine Way	A 9	16	Langholme Dr.	B 4	10			
Irwin Av.	H 4	13	Lansdowne Ter.	H 6	13	Lower Ebor St.	F 6	12
Iver Clo.	B 5	10	Larchfield	K 3	9	Lower Friargate	F 6	5

Street	Ref		Street	Ref		Street	Ref	
Lower Priory St.	F 6	4	Melwood Gro.	A 4	10	Murton Way	M 5	15
Loweswater Rd.	C 2	6	Merchant Gate	G 6	5	Museum St.	F 5	4
Lowfield La.	A 5	10	Merlin Ct.	H 1	8			
Lowfields Dr.	B 6	10	Micklegate	F 6	4	Nairn Clo.	B 9	16
Lowick	B 9	16	Micklegate Bar	F 6	4	Navigation Rd.	G 5	5
Lown Hill	B 7	16	Middleham Av.	H 2	8	Nelson St.	G 4	13
Lowther St.	G 4	13	Middlethorpe Dr.	D 9	17	Nelsons La.	D 8	17
Lowther Ter.	E 6	4	Middlethorpe Gro.	D 9	17	Nessgate	F 5	5
Lucas Av.	F 3	7	Middleton Rd.	B 7	16	Neville St.	G 4	13
Lumley Rd.	E 3	7	Mildred Gro.	D 7	17	Neville Ter.	G 4	13
Lycett Rd.	D 9	17	Mill Gates	B 4	10	Nevinson Gro.	H 8	19
Lydham Ct.	B 8	16	Mill La.	H 4	13	Nevis Way	A 9	16
Lyndale Av.	L 6	15	Mill Mount Ct.	E 6	12	New La.	D 6	11
Lynden Way	C 6	11	Mill Mt.	E 6	12	New St.	F 5	4
			Mill St.	G 6	5	New Walk Ter.	G 7	19
Maida Gro.	G 7	19	Millfield Av.	J 6	14	New Wk.	G 7	19
Main Av.	H 4	13	Millfield La.	J 6	14	Newborough St.	F 4	12
Main St.	K 7	20	Millfield Rd.	F 7	18	Newbury Av.	C 7	17
Malham Gro.	K 5	14	Milner St.	C 6	11	Newby Ter.	F 3	7
Malton Av.	H 4	13	Milson Gro.	J 6	14	Newgate	G 5	5
Malton Rd.	H 3	8	Milton Carr	D 2	6	Newland	J 6	14
Malton Way	D 3	6	Milton St.	H 6	13	Park Clo.		
Malvern Av.	C 5	11	Minster Av.	H 1	8	Newland Park Dr.	J 6	14
Manor Dr. N.	C 5	11	Minster Gates	F 5	5	Newlands Dr.	B 4	10
Manor Dr. S.	C 5	11	Minster Yd.	F 5	4	Newton Ter.	F 6	4
Manor La.	C 1	6	Mistral Ct.	G 3	8	Nicholas St.	H 6	13
Manor Park Clo.	C 1	6	Mitchels La.	J 8	20	Nidd Gro.	C 9	17
Manor Park Gro.	C 1	6	Miterdale	B 9	16	Nigel Gro.	D 7	17
Manor Park Rd.	C 1	6	Moat Field	L 5	15	Ninth Av.	H 5	13
Manor Way	C 1	6	Moatside Ct.	F 5	4	Norfolk St.	F 7	18
Mansfield St.	G 5	5	Monk Av.	H 3	8	Norman Dr.	A 4	10
Manthorpe Wk.	C 5	11	Monkgate	G 5	5	Norman St.	J 6	14
Maple Ct.	G 1	8	Monkgate Cloisters	G 5	5	North La.	C 8	17
Maple Gro.	G 8	19	Monkton Rd.	H 3	8	North Par.	E 4	12
Maplewood Paddock	B 8	16	Montague St.	F 8	18	North St.	F 5	4
			Moor Gro.	D 8	17	Northcote Av.	D 6	11
March St.	G 4	13	Moor La., Acomb Park	A 9	16	Northfield Ter.	C 8	17
Margaret St.	G 6	5				Northolme Dr.	D 2	6
Market St.	F 5	4	Moor La., Woodthorpe	C 9	17	Nunmill St.	F 7	18
Markham Cres.	G 4	13				Nunnery La.	F 6	4
Markham St.	G 4	13	Moor Lea Av.	C 8	17	Nunthorpe Av.	F 7	18
Marlborough Gro.	G 7	19	Moorcroft Rd.	C 9	17	Nunthorpe Cres.	F 7	18
Marston Av.	A 6	10	Moore Av.	K 5	14	Nunthorpe Dr.	F 7	18
Marston Cres.	A 6	10	Moorgarth Av.	D 7	17	Nunthorpe Gdns.	F 7	18
Martin Cheeseman Ct.	B 8	16	Moorgate	C 6	11	Nunthorpe Gro.	F 7	18
			Moorland Rd.	G 8	19	Nunthorpe Rd.	F 6	12
Marygate	F 5	4	Moorside Ct.	F 4	12	Nunthorpe Vw.	F 7	18
Marygate La.	F 5	4	Morrell Ct.	B 8	16	Nursery Dr.	C 6	11
Mattison Way	C 7	17	Morritt Clo.	H 2	8	Nursery Gdns.	L 6	15
Mayfield Gro.	D 8	17	Moss St.	E 6	4			
Maythorn Rd.	H 1	8	Mount Ephraim	E 6	12	Oak Glade	H 1	8
Meadlands	K 4	14	Mount Par.	E 6	12	Oak St.	C 5	11
Meadow Way	J 3	9	Mount Vale	E 7	18	Oak Tree Gro.	G 1	8
Meadowfields Dr.	G 1	8	Mount Vale Dr.	E 7	18	Oakland Av.	J 3	9
Melander Clo.	A 5	10	Mount, The	E 6	12	Oakland Dr.	J 4	14
Melbourne St.	G 6	13	Mowbray Dr.	B 5	10	Oakville St.	G 3	8
Melrose Clo.	J 5	14	Muirfield Way	A 5	10	Ogleforth	G 5	5
Melrosegate	J 4	14	Mulwith Clo.	J 4	14	Old Moor La.	C 9	17
Melroses Yd.	G 6	5	Muncastergate	H 3	8	Old Orchard, The	H 9	19
Melton Av.	D 2	6	Murray St.	D 6	11	Oldman Ct.	B 8	16
Melton Dr.	D 2	6	Murrough Wilson Pl.	F 3	7	Orchard Clo.	C 8	17

Name	Ref	Name	Ref	Name	Ref
Orchard Gdns.	H 1 8	Pinelands Way	L 6 15	Riverside Wk.	F 5 4
Orchard Way	C 8 17	Pinewood Gro.	H 1 8	Robin Gro.	D 6 11
Ordnance La.	G 7 19	Pinewood Hill	L 6 15	Robinson Dr.	A 7 16
Oriel Gro.	E 2 7	Pinfold Ct.	E 3 7	Roche Av.	H 2 8
Orrin Clo.	B 9 16	Plantation Dr.	B 4 10	Rockingham Av.	J 5 14
Osbaldwick La.	K 5 14	Plantation Gro.	B 4 10	Rogers Ct.	B 8 16
Osbaldwick Village	L 5 15	Plumer Av.	J 5 14	Rolston Av.	H 1 8
Osprey Clo.	A 8 16	Poplar Gro.	G 1 8	Rose St.	G 3 8
Ostman Rd.	B 5 10	Poplar St.	C 5 11	Rosebery St.	D 4 11
Otterwood Bank	A 8 16	Poppleton Rd.	C 5 11	Rosedale Av.	B 6 10
Otterwood La.	A 8 16	Portal Rd.	A 4 10	Rosedale St.	G 7 19
Ouse Acres	C 4 11	Portland St.	F 4 12	Rosemary Ct.	G 5 5
Ouse Lea	E 3 7	Pottery La.	G 3 8	Rosemary Pl.	G 5 5
Ouseburn Av.	B 4 10	Precentors Ct.	F 5 4	Rosslyn St.	E 4 12
Ousecliffe Gdns.	E 4 12	Price St.	F 6 12	Rougier St.	F 5 4
Overdale Clo.	B 9 16	Prices La.	F 6 4	Rowntree Av.	F 3 7
Ovington Ter.	E 7 18	Priors Wk.	C 4 11	Ruby St.	E 7 18
Owston Av.	J 6 14	Priory St.	F 6 4	Runswick Av.	A 6 10
Oxford St.	E 6 12	Priory Wood Way	H 1 8	Russell St.	F 7 18
		Prospect Ter.	F 6 4	Russet Dr.	K 5 14
Paddock Way	B 4 10	Prospect Ter., Fulford	G 9 19	Rydal Av.	J 4 14
Paddock, The	B 4 10			Ryecroft Av.	B 9 16
Palace Vw.	G 9 19	Pulleyn Dr.	D 7 17	Ryecroft Clo.	K 3 9
Palmer La.	G 5 5			Rylatt Pl.	A 6 10
Paragon St.	G 6 5	Quaker Grn.	B 9 16		
Park Cres.	G 4 13	Queen Annes Rd.	E 4 4	Sadberge Ct.	K 6 14
Park Ct.	J 4 14	Queen St.	E 6 4	Saddlebrook Ct.	B 8 16
Park Gro.	G 4 13	Queen Victoria St.	E 7 18	St. Andrewgate	G 5 5
Park La.	D 6 11	Queens Path, The	G 5 5	St. Andrews Ct.	G 5 5
Park St.	E 6 4	Queens Staith	F 6 4	St. Annes Ct.	G 6 13
Parker Av.	A 7 16	Queens Staith Ms.	F 6 4	St. Aubyns Pl.	E 7 18
Parkside Clo.	C 6 11	Queens Staith Rd.	F 6 4	St. Benedict Rd.	F 6 12
Parliament St.	F 5 5	Queenswood Gro.	C 7 17	St. Catherines Pl.	E 6 12
Paston Wk.	F 6 12			St. Clements Gro.	F 7 18
Pasture Farm Clo.	G 9 19	Railway Ter.	E 6 12	St. Denys Rd.	G 6 5
Pasture La.	K 3 9	Railway Vw.	C 8 17	St. Edwards Clo.	D 8 17
Pastures, The	D 8 17	Ratcliffe St.	F 3 7	St. Georges Pl.	D 7 17
Pately Pl.	C 6 11	Raven Gro.	B 5 10	St. Helens Rd.	D 8 17
Patrick Pool	F 5 5	Rawcliffe Av.	D 3 6	St. Helens Sq.	F 5 4
Patterdale Dr.	C 2 6	Rawcliffe Clo.	C 1 6	St. James Mt.	E 7 18
Pavement	G 5 5	Rawcliffe Croft	C 1 6	St. James Pl.	C 8 17
Paver La.	G 6 5	Rawcliffe Dr.	E 3 7	St. Johns Cres.	G 4 13
Pear Tree Ct.	G 5 5	Rawcliffe Gro.	D 3 6	St. Johns St.	G 4 5
Peasholme Grn.	G 5 5	Rawcliffe La.	D 2 6	St. Leonards Pl.	F 5 4
Peckitt St.	F 6 5	Rawcliffe Way	C 1 6	St. Lukes Gro.	F 3 7
Peel Clo.	J 8 20	Rawdon Av.	H 5 13	St. Margarets Ter.	G 6 5
Peel St.	G 6 5	Rectory Gdns.	F 7 18	St. Marks Gro.	C 1 6
Pembroke St.	F 3 7	Redcoat Way	A 8 16	St. Martins La.	F 6 4
Penleys Ct.	G 4 13	Redeness St.	G 5 5	St. Marys	F 5 4
Penleys Grove St.	G 4 13	Redthorn Dr.	H 2 8	St. Marys Clo.	L 6 15
Pennycourt La.	G 5 5	Reeves, The	B 7 16	St. Marys La.	F 5 4
Penyghent Av.	J 4 14	Regent St.	H 6 13	St. Marys Sq.	G 6 5
Percys La.	G 6 5	Reginald Gro.	F 8 18	St. Marys Ter.	F 5 4
Peter Hill Dr.	E 3 7	Reighton Av.	D 2 6	St. Maurices Rd.	G 5 5
Peter La.	F 5 5	Reighton Dr.	D 2 6	St. Nicholas Pl.	H 6 13
Petergate	F 5 12	Retreat, The	H 6 13	St. Olaves Rd.	F 4 12
Peters Way	E 4 12	Ribstone Gro.	K 4 14	St. Oswalds Rd.	G 8 19
Pheasant Dr.	B 8 16	Richardson St.	F 7 18	St. Pauls Sq.	E 6 12
Philadelphia Ter.	E 7 18	Richmond St.	H 5 13	St. Pauls Ter.	E 6 12
Piccadilly	G 5 5	Ridgeway	A 6 10	St. Peters Gro.	E 4 12
Pilgrim St.	F 4 12	River St.	F 6 12	St. Phillips Gro.	E 3 7

Street	Ref		Street	Ref		Street	Ref	
St. Sampsons Sq.	F 5	5	Skiddaw	B 9	16	Sykes Clo.	F 4	12
St. Saviourgate	G 5	5	Slessor Rd.	A 8	16			
St. Saviours Pl.	G 5	5	Slingsby Gro.	D 9	17	Tadcaster Rd.	D 9	17
St. Stephens Rd.	B 7	16	Smales St.	F 6	4	Tang Hall La.	J 4	14
St. Stephens Sq.	B 7	16	Smeaton Gro.	B 5	10	Tanner Row	F 5	4
St. Swithins Wk.	C 6	11	Somerset Rd.	G 3	8	Tanners Moat	F 5	4
St. Thomas Pl.	G 4	13	South Bank Av.	F 7	18	Tarbert Cres.	A 9	16
St. Thomass Clo.	L 5	15	South Cotts.	C 2	6	Teck St.	F 6	12
Salisbury Rd.	D 4	11	South Esplanade	F 6	5	Tedder Rd.	A 7	16
Salisbury Ter.	D 4	11	South Par.	E 6	4	Telford Ter.	E 7	18
Salmond Rd.	B 8	16	South View Ter.	B 6	10	Temple Av.	K 5	14
Sandcroft Clo.	C 8	17	Southfield Cres.	C 8	17	Templemead	H 3	8
Sandcroft Rd.	C 8	17	Southlands Rd.	F 7	18	Ten Thorn La.	A 5	10
Sandringham St.	G 7	19	Southolme Dr.	D 2	6	Tennent Rd.	B 7	16
Sandstock Rd.	K 3	9	Sowerby Rd.	C 5	11	Tennyson Av.	F 3	7
Saville Gro.	E 2	7	Spalding Av.	E 3	7	Terry Av.	F 6	5
Saxon Pl.	G 3	8	Speculation St.	G 6	5	Terry Av.	G 7	19
Scafell Clo.	C 2	6	Spen La.	G 5	5	Terry St.	F 8	18
Scaife St.	G 3	8	Spey Bank	B 9	16	Thackerays Yd.	G 6	5
Scarborough Ter.	F 4	12	Spinney, The	D 9	17	Thanet Rd.	C 8	17
Scarcroft Hill	E 7	18	Springfield Clo.	K 3	9	Thief La.	H 6	13
Scarcroft La.	F 6	4	Springfield Way	K 3	9	Third Av.	H 4	13
Scarcroft Rd.	E 6	12	Spurr Ct.	B 8	16	Thirkleby Way	L 5	15
Scawton Av.	H 1	8	Spurriergate	F 5	4	Thirlmere Dr.	J 4	14
School La., Fulford	H 9	19	Staindale Clo.	D 1	6	Thomas St.	H 6	13
			Staithes Clo.	B 6	10	Thoresby Rd.	A 7	16
School La., Heslington	K 7	20	Stamford St. E.	D 5	11	Thorn Nook	H 3	8
			Stamford St. W.	D 5	11	Thornfield Av.	H 2	8
School St.	C 6	11	Stanley St.	G 4	13	Thornfield Dr.	H 1	8
Scott St.	F 7	18	Starkey Cres.	J 5	14	Thornwood Covert	B 8	16
Scrope Av.	H 5	13	Station Av.	F 5	4	Thorpe St.	F 7	18
Second Av.	H 4	13	Station Av., New Earswick	G 1	8	Tilmire Clo.	H 8	19
Sefton Av.	H 2	8				Tisbury Rd.	D 5	11
Segrave Wk.	C 5	11	Station Rd.	E 6	4	Tithe Clo.	A 7	16
Seldon Rd.	C 5	11	Station Ri.	F 5	4	Toft Grn.	F 6	4
Serton Close Av.	K 5	14	Sterne Av.	J 5	14	Torridon Pl.	A 9	16
Seventh Av.	H 5	13	Stirling Gro.	H 8	19	Tostig Av.	B 5	10
Severus Av.	C 5	11	Stirrup Clo.	A 8	16	Tower Pl.	F 6	5
Severus St.	C 6	11	Stockton La.	J 3	9	Tower St.	F 6	5
Seymour Gro.	H 4	13	Stonebow, The	G 5	5	Townend St.	F 4	12
Shallowdale Gro.	L 6	15	Stonegate	F 5	4	Towton Av.	D 7	17
Shambles	G 5	5	Stonelands Ct.	E 2	7	Trafalgar St.	F 7	18
Shaws Ter.	E 6	4	Stones Clo.	C 7	17	Tranby Av.	L 5	15
Shelley Gro.	D 2	6	Stonethwaite	B 9	16	Trenchard Rd.	A 4	10
Sherringham Dr.	B 8	16	Stray Garth	H 3	8	Trent Way	C 9	17
Sherwood Gro.	A 4	10	Stray Rd.	K 4	14	Trentholme Dr.	E 7	18
Sherwood Gro., New Earswick	H 1	8	Straylands Gro.	J 3	9	Trevor Gro.	D 6	11
			Stuart Rd.	C 7	17	Trinity La.	F 6	4
Shipton Rd.	C 1	6	Sturdee Ct.	G 3	8	Troutbeck	B 9	16
Shipton St.	F 3	7	Summerfield Rd.	B 9	16	Troutsdale Av.	C 1	6
Shirley Av.	B 4	10	Surtees St.	F 3	7	Tudor Rd.	B 7	16
Silver St.	F 5	5	Sussex Clo.	K 7	20	Tuke Av.	K 5	14
Silverdale Ct.	B 9	16	Sussex Rd.	K 7	20	Turners Croft	J 8	20
Sirocco Ct.	G 3	8	Sutherland St.	E 8	18	Turnmire Rd.	C 8	17
Sitwell Gro.	B 4	10	Sutton Way	F 2	7			
Siward St.	J 6	14	Swale Av.	C 8	17	Ullswater	B 9	16
Sixth Av.	H 5	13	Swann St.	F 6	4	Union Ter.	F 4	12
Skeldergate	F 6	4	Swinegate	F 5	5	University Rd.	J 7	20
Skeldergate Bri.	F 6	5	Swinerton Av.	D 4	11	Upper Hanover St.	D 5	11
Skelton Ct.	E 4	12	Sycamore Pl.	E 5	4	Upper Newborough St.	F 3	7
Skewsby Gro.	H 2	8	Sycamore Ter.	E 5	4			

Name	Grid		Name	Grid		Name	Grid	
Upper Price St.	F 6	12	Welton Av.	C 4	11	William Plows Av.	H 6	13
Upper St. Pauls Ter.	E 6	12	Welwyn Dr.	H 8	19	Willis St.	G 6	13
			Wenlock Ter.	G 7	19	Willoughby Way	B 8	16
			Wentworth Rd.	E 7	18	Willow Bank	G 1	8
Vanbrugh Dr.	L 6	15	Werkdyke	G 5	5	Willow Glade	H 1	8
Vernon Rd.	C 1	6	West Bank	C 6	11	Willow Gro.	J 3	9
Vesper Dr.	B 6	10	West Moor La.	J 8	20	Wilsthorpe Gro.	H 8	19
Victor St.	F 6	4	West Thorpe	C 8	17	Wilton Ri.	D 6	11
Victoria Bar	F 6	4	Westerdale Ct.	E 4	12	Winchester Av.	C 5	11
Viking Rd.	B 5	10	Westfield Dr.	G 8	19	Winchester Gro.	C 5	11
Villa Gro.	H 4	13	Westfield Pl.	A 7	16	Windermere	C 9	17
Village St.	A 5	10	Westholme Dr.	C 2	6	Windmill La.	K 6	14
Vincent Way	B 8	16	Westlands Gro.	J 3	9	Windmill Ri.	D 6	11
Vine St.	F 7	18	Westminster Rd.	E 4	12	Windsor Garth	C 7	17
Vyner St.	F 3	7	Westview Clo.	A 4	10	Windsor St.	E 7	18
			Westwood Ter.	E 8	18	Winterscale St.	G 7	19
Wains Gro.	C 9	17	Wetherby Rd.	A 6	10	Wolfe Av.	J 5	14
Wains Rd.	C 8	17	Wharfe Dr.	C 8	17	Wolsley St.	H 6	13
Wainsbeck	A 9	16	Wharton Av.	E 3	7	Wolviston Av.	K 6	14
Walker Dr.	B 8	16	Wheatlands Gro.	B 4	10	Wood St.	H 4	13
Walmgate	G 6	5	Whenby Gro.	H 2	8	Woodford Pl.	C 7	17
Walmgate Bar	G 6	5	Whernside Av.	J 4	14	Woodhouse Gro.	J 5	14
Walney Rd.	J 4	14	Whin Clo.	D 9	17	Woodlands Gro.	J 3	9
Walpole St.	G 3	8	Whin Garth	D 9	17	Woodlea Av.	B 5	10
Walton Pl.	A 6	10	Whin Rd.	D 9	17	Woodlea Bank	B 5	10
Walworth St.	D 4	11	Whip-Ma-Whop-Ma-Gate	G 5	5	Woodlea Cres.	B 5	10
Wandle, The	A 7	16				Woodlea Gro.	B 5	10
Ward Ct.	F 6	12	Whitby Av.	J 3	9	Woodside Av.	J 4	14
Warwick St.	G 4	13	Whitby Dr.	J 3	9	Woolnough Av.	K 6	14
Wasdale Clo.	C 2	6	White Cross Rd.	G 3	8	Worcester Dr.	K 4	14
Water End	C 5	11	White House Dale	D 7	17	Wordsworth Cres.	B 9	16
Water La.	E 3	7	White House Dr.	D 7	17	Wrays Av.	H 2	8
Watson St.	E 6	12	White House Gdns.	D 7	17	Wrays Cotts.	H 2	8
Watson Ter.	E 6	12				Wycliffe Av.	K 6	14
Waveney Gro.	F 2	7	White House Ri.	D 7	17	Wydale Rd.	L 5	15
Waverley St.	G 4	13	White Rose Av.	G 1	8			
Waynefleet Gro.	J 6	14	White Rose Gro.	G 1	8	Yarburgh Gro.	C 5	11
Weddall Clo.	D 8	17	Whitethorn Clo.	H 1	8	Yarburgh Way	L 6	15
Welborn Clo.	J 5	14	Whitton Pl.	K 6	14	Yearsley Cres.	G 3	8
Welland Ri.	C 5	11	Wigginton Rd.	F 1	7	Yearsley Gro.	H 2	8
Wellington Row	F 5	4	Wigginton Ter.	F 3	7	Yew Tree Mews	L 5	15
Wellington St.	G 6	13	Wilberforce Av.	F 3	7	York Rd.	B 6	10

ADDENDUM

Name	Grid		Name	Grid		Name	Grid	
Alder Way	G1	8	Ferguson Way	J2	9	Juniper Clo.	G1	8
Andrew Dr.	H2	8	Fewston Dr.	D2	6	Kathryn Av.	K1	9
Angram Clo.	D2	6	Geldof Rd.	H2	8	Kettlestring La.	D1	6
Barden Ct.	D2	6	George Cayley Dr.	E1	7	Lancaster Way	E2	7
Beaver Dyke	D2	6	Halifax Ct.	E2	7	Lanshaw Cft.	D2	6
Birch Clo.	G1	8	Harrow Glade	E2	7	Leighton Cft.	D2	6
Bransholme Dr.	E1	7	Hastings Clo.	E2	7	Loxley Clo.	D1	6
Chelkar Way	D2	6	Hendon Garth	E2	7	Oakdale Rd.	D1	6
Clifton Moor Gate	D1	6	Ilton Garth	E1	7	Rishworth Gro.	D1	6
Dalby Mead	H2	8	James Nicholson Link	D1	6	Ryburn Clo.	D1	6
Ebsay Dr.	D2	6	Jockey La.	J1	9	Swinsty Ct.	D2	6
Eldwick Clo.	D2	6	Julia Av.	K1	9			